WHAT'S YOUR CATALYST?

The Power of Managed Change

What's Your CATALYST?
The Power of Managed Change

How Purpose and Passion Can Drive Strategic Life Change

BY ALANA M. HILL, PMP

Cover design by Expressionistic Designs
Photography by Doss Tidwell
Edited by: Elite Authors

To my husband, Rodney. My biggest supporter and partner in all of life's journey.

To my oldest son, Malcolm. May your loving memory continue to surround our family.

To my younger sons Marcus, Mason, and Matthew. You guys remind me daily of what matters most. I'm grateful and proud to be part of the men you are becoming.

Preface

. . .

Life is full of change. Sometimes change happens to us, and sometimes change happens because of us. What I've found in my years as a wife, mom, and project-management consultant is that we all need help adapting to change. But more importantly, we need tools to help us lead change—tools that include setting and achieving our goals. Have you ever noticed accomplished professionals with chaotic personal lives or people who manage change well at home but create disorder at work? Often the reason for that is people don't reinforce their goals with purpose and passion.

I wrote this book because I saw a need to create a resource to help professionals excel in both their personal lives and their careers without sacrificing one or the other. In my twenty-plus-year career as an international project and change manager, I have had the privilege of leading people and projects that spanned industries, continents, and functions. Above all, what I'm most proud of is raising my four handsome boys to be men of faith while I did it. I can't say that I've seen it all, but boy, I've seen a lot. I operate by the proverb "As iron sharpens iron, so one man sharpens another."

It's not by accident that I learned some of the most powerful personal growth techniques while leading process-optimization projects. The parallels jumped out at me daily, and I developed a critical eye for excellence in myself and others. It wasn't until I became fully immersed in my faith that I encountered the compassion needed to properly apply those techniques to my life, career, family, and community. The result is a simple methodology to manage life change with the same excellence and empathy that is required to lead change in Fortune 500 companies: leading change... the Ms. Engineer Way!

To consistently navigate and lead change in your life and in your organization, you need a set of skills and tools along with a pressing reason. In this book, I will teach you how to identify that reason, which is your catalyst. From there, you will learn how to work strategically while carefully analyzing your current state and using that information to drive incremental development plans. You will find that your plans succeed more often, and, in turn, so do you.

Most people who use project-management skills are not project managers. For that reason, this book simplifies project strategy, planning, and execution so that you can apply it to any project—including your life!

Get ready to become a more effective and resilient change leader at work and at home.

Contents

Acknowledgments

· · ·

I am giving th anks to my Creator first because without him, I am nothing. He has blessed me with so much love, and my faith is foundational to my being. I am so grateful for the support and encouragement of my family, especially my husband, Rodney. Additionally, I have received an abundance of support and guidance from several people. I will name a few.

First, thank you to Rick A. Morris, PMP, for encouraging me at the Project Management Institute (PMI) Houston conference where we met all those years ago. He was the opening keynote speaker, and I was an overzealous audience member Not only did I meet Rick on the day my oldest son, Malcolm, rang the cancer-free bell, but I also received immediate, actionable advice on how to become an author and speaker. Thanks, Rick!

Thank you to my mentors, colleagues, and clients who have stretched me and helped me to be a better leader by setting the standard at every turn: Paula McCann Harris; Francesco Turchetti; Walter Viali, PMP; Don James, PMP; and Beth Green—2Hill Consulting Services would not be the success it is without your early and continued support.

When I heard the call to speak, I went to the altar, and then I joined the National Speakers Association (NSA). There, I met some of the most incredible, supportive, and encouraging people on the planet. I can't thank them all, but I have to give special thanks to Mike Lejeune; Liz Meyers; Amy Castro; Delatorro McNeal II, CSP; and Ed Robinson, CSP. And thank you to every speaker who hugged me at my first NSA Influence conference. The spirit of NSA founder Cavett Roberts is alive and well!

Thank you to all who have heard and participated in the workshops that helped formulate this material. Your presence and participation added richness.

Thank you to my incredible team for completing this project. You guys are the best. And finally, thank you to my readers for your interest in what I have to say.

Finding My Catalyst: *The* Africa Story

• • •

Ten years into my career in oil and gas working as an engineer and program manager with the oil-field services company Schlumberger, I received an assignment to conduct a service quality audit. It would require me to travel to Malabo, the capital of Central Africa's Equatorial Guinea, and Douala, the leading commercial and economic hub of Cameroon. Little did my Dutch audit team manager, Eddy, realize at the time, visiting these sub-Saharan African nations was, for me, the fulfillment of a personal dream.

I remember the moment when the overhead chimed with a loud *ding!* followed by the pilot's voice on the speaker: "You are now free to move about the cabin." My heart raced, and my stomach fluttered as I thought about our destination. You see, although I had traveled internationally many times before, I had never been to sub-Saharan Africa. This exact moment ignited the essence of my long-awaited dream of traveling to a new and exciting place where I could not only do my job as an auditor and knowledge-management facilitator but also discover my roots and wiggle my toes in Central African soil.

During the flight, I closed my eyes and visualized the island's tropical setting, the breathtaking Venus Bay, and the colonial architecture that Malabo is so famous for. I looked forward to working amid the wonder of a people and a land where Westernization meets Africanism. I dozed off into dreams of discovering the motherland. I proudly wore my Woman of Africa T-shirt that I had purchased when I was in college, looking the part of an eager African American tourist.

I knew that there would also be grueling moments, such as when our team of managers from all around the world would have to come down a bit tough on the team in Malabo. After all, the job of the auditor is to analyze what they are doing wrong and what they need to do to improve and achieve success for the company. We had flown into Malabo to complete a specific mission, and we had positioned ourselves to do our jobs well. "Stop doing that! Do it this way," we would demand.

Our job was to go in, point fingers, question why people were delayed in their training, and compel them to provide us with viable answers as to why that was the case. We prepared ourselves to go in as a well-organized team and establish both our knowledge and our authority over the situation.

After all, our dashboard showed that they were behind in implementing certain processes and failed to keep up with proposed deadlines. They were behind on the objectives, some of which I had established. We needed to focus them on excellence and push them to work faster and more efficiently. After spending a lot of money on engineers and technicians, our number one question would be "Why are you delayed?"

My reputation was on the line.

Thus, coached on how to pound my fist on a desk, I prepared to go out to the facility to discover the areas for improvement and determine how to address them to turn them around. The team and I would tell them that they needed to hurry up and finish their training. We would insist that adequate processes were put in place to ensure quality and client satisfaction. We would ensure that the employees in the location were properly adhering to the safety standards in order to reduce the likelihood of injury or accident. We would stress compliance. That was the plan.

I remember those initial moments in Malabo. We were in the capital city, not some remote village. It had internet and running water. Despite that, the weather was hot and humid—a breeding ground for mosquitoes carrying malaria. Nonetheless I breathed in the tropical air and prepared to be amazed at the wonders this West African island would provide.

My hosts, Craig and Colleen, a friendly couple from Louisiana, met me at the airport. They took me on a brief driving tour before heading to the staff housing.

Shock overwhelmed me as I watched half-dressed (and even some naked) children drawing buckets of dirty water to take back home. One little boy carrying a big, red bucket on his head remained in my line of sight as we drove down the dusty, gravel road. Colleen explained that there was a cholera outbreak. It is usually contracted when an individual drinks dirty and infected water, the kind of dirty water that these precious, naked babies were carrying home. Cholera is a disease that can be completely eradicated. Yet here, in our modern times, when medical advancements had achieved so much, it still existed. Colleen explained that it was taking a toll on the children.

I wondered why more hadn't been done to stop the outbreak.

The more I saw, the more I realized that this was an impoverished town disguised as an emerging city. There were oil wells and residents who gained wealth because of this oil, but the town itself was racked with poverty, suffering, and deadly disease. The locals were composed of starving families and expatriates who exploited young girls.

While we were touring the city, my hosts filled me in on the social, political, and spiritual climate of the city we were in. For example, we were not allowed to take photos because the president forbade it. One of my only souvenirs is a blurry picture I took out the window as I tried to capture the palm trees and ocean as we drove by.

Our drive was interrupted by a presidential motorcade. The contrast of lifestyles was mind-blowing. As we passed the crudely built shanties that people lived in, the motorcade of fine black Mercedes, Escalades, and Expeditions approached. We were first directed to pull over to the side of the road and then forced to get out of the car. Armed members of the president's security detail held us at gunpoint as the cars passed. Many attempts had been made on the president's life. Seeing the obvious contrast in lifestyles coupled with the suffering and withholding of resources, I understood why. Equatorial Guinea was an oil-rich nation. However, due to the corruption, the people didn't benefit from it very much.

As we passed by a church, I saw a line of young girls with looks of humiliation on their faces as oil-field workers came through. I would later learn that most of these precious girls had been forced into prostitution, many as early as twelve years old. How unfortunate that they would be staged in front of a church.

I also noticed separate housing units that consisted of dilapidated shacks for the locals and a sprawling housing development for expatriates, which included my international team and me. Our house mother, a Malabo local, was pregnant. I was holding a copy of Beth Moore's *Believing God*. I started to barrage her with the usual "mommy" questions: "When are you due? Is this your first? How many children do you—"?

Before I could finish my question, I froze. I dared not ask more questions about her family because I feared that her stories might be too sad for her to endure. As I thought of the little boy with the red bucket and the fact that cholera had claimed the lives of so many children before their second birthday, my heart broke for this beautiful, young mother.

As she and I talked, she explained to me that she was pregnant with her third child. Our eyes met, and I knew there was more to that story. She filled me in on details about her husband and those who worked security for the staff housing. She explained that they monitored the house around the clock, rain or shine.

I felt helpless as I took it all in. I thought about how, even though I was in a good place that included new directions with my family and a flourishing career, my faith was leading me in a different direction. Although I was in Malabo conducting business, my heart led me to talk to this woman. Thus, while I was there, operating in obedience to my company to do what I was told to do, I realized that I had been called to do something different.

Equatorial Guinea was colonized first by the British, Portuguese, and later by the Spaniards, leaving Spanish as its official language. Armed with my high school Spanish and practice from my time working in south Texas, I was able to communicate with the staff and conduct the audit (this involved a lot of gestures and charades, but I made it through). As I questioned why they had not complied with their required self-study training, a colleague informed me that the local workers went home to dirt floors with no electricity or running water. Suddenly the bus full of the same laborers I had seen the day before looked familiar; they were employed by the same company I worked for, yet they had far less to show for their efforts. I had missed that element in my needs assessment. That ball of emotions sat with me for a while.

Every morning our team started in a manager's office and shared notes from the day before. We would start with infractions, and our discussions always evolved into a review of the people we interacted with. Two of the audit team members were expatriates working in other West African countries, so the exchanges managed to give me insight into the entire region—talk about the world coming to life!

We would head back to the staff house for lunch, and Colleen would prepare us a delicious buffet. We would eat quickly, take a nap, and freshen up for the rest of the day. We had a lot of ground to cover, and the hours were long.

Each night was a different dining experience. One night, we ate in the only Chinese restaurant in town (which only had two tables), and when it got dark, the bats, mosquitoes, and prostitutes all came out. We found another local restaurant with a pool table, and our team had some time to unwind and decompress from the day's events.

We closed the audit with a summary presentation delivered by the best Spanish speaker on our team: me. I sounded like a third grader, but we made our way through. Oh, if only I had taken one more year of Spanish!

After three days in Malabo, our team said goodbye to our hosts and headed to Douala. The city is known for its great West African artists, museums that depict the country's history, and a proliferation of native elephants and crocodiles. More than 75 percent of Cameroon's industry is located in Douala. Once we arrived, we had some free time to eat at one of Douala's finer restaurants and do a little shopping. I purchased a large, mahogany elephant to put in my office next to the small ones I had received from a colleague a few years prior.

Although the standard of living is considerably higher than Equatorial Guinea, it is still considerably lower than what we have here in the United States. In Cameroon, more than half of the inhabitants live below the poverty line. While most of the impoverished live in the rural areas, much of Douala is still undeveloped. Roads and infrastructures are both poor and largely underdeveloped. Despite the dirt roads, however, I saw a group of people running in the early morning hours, joyfully chanting as they went along. I saw three people riding on a motorcycle on their way to work.

The audit of this location revealed a similar paradox to the other one. I didn't experience the living conditions of the employees, but I sensed that they, like the Malabo crews, were barely providing for their families. I visited the manager's home one night because he made arrangements for me to have my hair braided. His was a modest but well-appointed home. On the drive there and back, I passed numerous shanty houses and even animals wandering freely. However, a few modern conveniences did exist, and I had internet in my hotel room. I emailed family and friends about my experiences in West Africa thus far.

Where in the World Is Alana?

At that point in my life, my standard practice when I felt inspired was to write. I journaled my thoughts, checked on family, and shared family news. When I traveled, I played a silly email game with my family and friends called Where in the World Is Alana? Despite my occasional travels, I was also a devoted wife and mother. My husband, Rodney, and I created a blended family that, like most families, required creative ways to keep us strong. These emails were one of my creative ways to stay connected with my husband as well as our extended family. I shared quips and anecdotes about my travels and various landing spots around the world. For example, in one of my emails, I posed the question, "Did you know that Equatorial Guinea is the only Spanish-speaking nation in Africa?" I shared photos of exotic locations and gave family and friends opportunities to ask questions and even guess where I was. It was a fun way to connect with my family and ease my longing to be back at home with them.

The arrangement for most of my business trips was to get in and get out. This trip to Africa was different, however, and required me to make multiple stops in a variety of countries over ten days. My trip began in Paris, where I worked with my manager and our team. I met Eddy, the audit team manager, at the Paris airport. We flew to Madrid for a night, then off to Malabo. We joined the rest of the audit team there and continued on to Douala, and from there I would fly home. The trip was beginning to take a toll on me. I missed my family terribly. Generally, my emails were positive and upbeat. It helped ease my homesickness and kept my family, especially my husband, from worry.

As I sat writing in a Cameroonian hotel room late one night, my tone was different. I wrote with a heavy heart. I described the toxic surroundings that confronted me. I cried as I chronicled the week's revelations: naked children lugging buckets of disease-infested water, the pregnant house mother who would soon be giving birth in squalid conditions, the poor technician who had no electricity or running water, and the young girls being forced to sell their bodies (even some in the lobby of the hotel I was in at the time). I closed one of my emails with a desperate plea that was disguised as a confession: "There's nothing I can do," I told them.

Then I hit send.

Moments later, I received a response from my uncle Lurie. "Or is there?" he asked simply.

His "Or is there?" response challenged my thinking and set off a chain of life-changing events. Totally impacted by my experiences in West Africa, I sent another email and expressed how I wanted to make a difference and a bigger impact.

I would hold myself accountable for the purpose and passion for life that I longed for. In my follow-up email to my family and friends, I wrote "Heavy Heart Clothes Drive" in the subject line. I urged them to send clothes and money to help the suffering African people.

When I returned home just a couple of days later, I forwarded the email to some colleagues and made flyers. We collected clothing for children and adults. That one email created enough interest to fill my entire living room with donated items! This posed a new challenge, as sending the items would be very expensive. So I said a prayer, made some calls, and was able to send the supplies on cargo vessels. My hosts on the ground coordinated the distribution through the church and local staff in Malabo. We even sent rain gear for the security workers. The message I took from that is

"Never underestimate the power of what you can do—even in an email!"

Before I left for Africa, I had been reluctant to go because of malaria. Even though I had received all the required antimalaria pills and other shots, I was still scared of getting sick. It didn't help that Eddy had actually contracted malaria before and scared me with his story. I realized that what was originally meant to be an audit to improve our company's processes revealed a much different purpose, which was to uplift hurting people. My worries became insignificant, and I pushed ahead anyway.

My college dreams of traveling to Africa were not so that I could wiggle my toes in African soil or feel the warm waters of Venus Bay on my skin; they were so that I could realize my gifts and use them to serve others. My job had sent me on a business trip, but my faith had sent me on a journey of self-discovery that would ultimately unveil my purpose. I had to confront myself and refocus my life.

What Matters Most

When I got back from that trip after having been gone for ten days, I was a changed person. My boys were thirteen, nine, six, and two. Every day that I spent away from them made me ache. That had been the longest business trip away from my family since its formation just five years prior (when I said, "I do, I do, I do, I do!" and, in a moment, became a wife and mom of three boys). Leading up to the trip, I was already reflecting on my priorities and searching for my purpose. I had significantly reduced my travel, and I had read Rick Warren's *The Purpose Driven Life*. I volunteered at church, but I didn't have time to be more involved in leadership, though I knew I was being called. I had invested time, energy, and emotion into getting healed and whole so that I could leave a legacy of love for my boys, but I still had work to do so that I could give of myself freely.

My memoir, *Love Is a Catalyst: The Pain behind the Purpose*, describes my journey to spiritual growth and healing from childhood trauma so that I could lead my children with purpose. Yet with each stroke of the pen, it became more evident that my purpose and position go hand in hand. I knew that overcoming adversity to become an engineer and international project manager (in oil and gas no less) were not separate from my desire to show love and compassion at home and in the workplace.

What lay ahead for me was a mission to combine my willingness to love even the most difficult people with the critical thinking, problem solving, and strategic planning I was touted for at work. It was time to make a change. It was time to leverage my strengths for a greater purpose. It was time to transform my life so that it reflected the priorities in my heart of faith, family, and my career. It was time to ask myself, "What's your catalyst?"

I was ready to unleash the power of managed change.

When I returned from Africa, I had been changed. The long braids that I was able to get in Cameroon offered only a physical glimpse of the deeper change that had occurred in my heart. I came back changed because I had started to look at what I viewed then as the paradox of being a successful project manager and doing what I was called to do. I had to ask myself, "How can I do both?"

That awakening occurred in April 2005.

The events that occurred in 2005 challenged me to question what matters most to me. Being able to spearhead the clothing drive allowed me to see the impact I could have. I saw that my actions could benefit not just my family but the world. I could not sit still any longer. I felt empowered and catalyzed for change.

I realized that I wanted to make room and time for what I was called to do. I had always insisted on owning my career so that I could manage my work-life balance. I set those goals not only because of the absence of my parents during my upbringing but also because of the intense stirring in my spirit indicating that it was time for me to become an even more engaged and involved mom.

My present work environment interfered far too much in my family life; I didn't miss field trips or important functions, but the daily routine was too hectic. I had a great arrangement with my previous manager; I was able to work from home twice a week, lead a team, and make a difference at home. But after returning from maternity leave a year prior, I was transferred to another department. This new manager was not as flexible, and we didn't get along very well. To make matters worse, the role I was given was less appealing than the one I had before. I worked to make the role more valuable, but the relationship was still full of contention. The stress and strife overwhelmed me. I struggled to leave my child at day care so that I could go to a job and work environment I did not love. My performance didn't waiver, but it took an excessive amount of energy to excel in this environment.

Every family is different, and ours was a blended, dual-career family. My husband, Rodney, had a demanding career in finance (also at the same company), and we both agreed that my leaving the company would be the solution to our family's current dilemma.

I resigned at the end of 2005 for the primary benefit of being able to spend more time with my family. I didn't want to be a working mom; I wanted to be a mom who worked. I also longed to have my own business for the autonomy it would give me in my career, but I had no idea how to go about doing so. I just knew that I'd had my last bad boss. Should I be my own boss? Should I find a different company? I had more questions than answers.

The transition terrified me.

I asked myself, "What should I do next?"

That question requires people to think critically about what motivates them, to analyze decisions they have made, and to consider events in their lives that have brought them to where they are thus far. It also forces people to think about decisions that they will make moving forward, requiring them to ponder not only about what they like and dislike but also about *why* they like and dislike certain things.

That question caused me to think about a transformation strategy. With an ample amount of savings and the support of my husband, I used my newfound freedom to evaluate what I wanted out of my life. I wanted to grow as a person, as a wife, as a mother, and as a professional.

Finding Your Catalyst

Change happens to us all. Disasters occur, companies downsize, and loved ones get sick. So many things happen beyond our control, but what about those things we can control? We have to plan strategically for our lives and use those plans to maximize our effectiveness. Because life is unpredictable, we also have to adjust those plans when the unexpected occurs. When you are faced with challenges, your catalyst will keep you focused on your goals and help you live a life that reflects your choices.

Today, as a change leadership expert, I love asking people, "What's your catalyst?"

In this book, I challenge you to discover your passions, talents, and path to being a more effective change leader at work and at home. You will dig deep and uncover who you are and who you were made to be. You will think critically about your life goals and create a strategy that will lead you to your desired outcome. This book and its online companion resources at www.WhatsYourCatalyst.com will leave you with a map to move you forward, along with an anchor for when the wind changes.

This book is divided into four sections that work together to help you create and sustain the priorities in your life:

- Part 1: Know Yourself

- Part 2: Make a Strategic Plan

- Part 3: Keep Your Focus

- Part 4: Sharpen Someone Else

Know Yourself

• • •

Knowing yourself is the beginning of all wisdom.

—Aristotle

There is great value in self-awareness. Before you embark on any change, it is important to first conduct a current state analysis, which means you need to know who you are today before you can transform into who you will be in the future.

To know yourself, you need to conduct a Know Yourself Assessment to identify your five key factors:

- Strengths

- Weaknesses

- Motivations

- Life Lessons

- Unique Purpose

CHAPTER 1

Know Your Strengths

• • •

Knowing yourself is the process of understanding who you are and what makes you tick on levels that extend beyond the surface. You need to know your strengths: what is it that you're good at doing naturally, and what strengths have you developed over time? You'll want to know how you can leverage your existing strengths while continuing to develop new ones.

Similar to knowing the current state of software before planning an upgrade, you have to be willing to analyze who you are currently before deciding who you are going to be. The engineers at Apple take careful note of the usefulness of an iPhone before planning the next version.

When I was growing up, my mother would always look at me and tell me that I was a better version of her. I lost my mother when I was in high school, so photographs and the memory of her affirmations of me are all that I have. As I work diligently to become a better version of me, I am, in turn, honoring her legacy. When I began the process of identifying my strengths, I had to first take inventory of where I excelled. I needed to define my strengths. I asked myself the question, "What are you good at doing?"

In my quest, I researched and used several reliable ways to determine my strengths. Some of them are costly and time consuming, while others are cost effective and relatively easy to use. For simplicity, I'll cover the three most valuable methods that will allow you to gain insight while not overanalyzing yourself.

There are numerous ways to get to know your strengths, but the three that I will focus on are completing a behavioral style assessment, discovering your natural gifts and talents, and asking people around you.

Behavioral Style Assessment

There are a variety of tools that can help you gain insight into your personality or behavioral style. These assessments reveal your preferences, motivations, and challenges when interacting with those around you. While the terms *personality* and *behavior* are often used interchangeably, they are different. Simply stated, personality is who you are (your thoughts, emotions, and behaviors), and it cannot be changed. Behavior is what you do, and it can be changed. For clarity, I will refer to your behavioral style in the context of managed change.

Many organizations utilize the Myers-Briggs Type Indicator (MBTI personality type). The assessment is based on the behavior, character, and individual trait profile identified by Swiss psychologist Dr. Carl Jung. It was adapted by the mother-daughter duo Katharine Briggs and Isabel Myers. One of the principles of the MBTI model is that each of us has an innate urge to grow, and part of our growth comes from understanding how we operate in the world. According to MBTI, by uncovering where we as individuals derive our energy, we can get a better sense of what comes naturally.

I had an opportunity to take the MBTI assessment in late 2000 when I was leading a team of information technology (IT) professionals and reporting to an eager visionary in the Talent Development Department. The assessment was part of a week-long seminar on leadership and interpersonal communication, and

I loved everything about it. I learned valuable leadership skills, and I saw my future as a consultant who facilitated change. It was, in fact, a turning point in my career when I began to envision what 2Hill Consulting would look like in the future. The seminar not only showed me my strengths but also helped me understand the strengths of people on my team, including my fun, inventive manager. I was equipped with information that would help me effectively lead and manage my team better. Training has always been my passion, and it showed me an ideal use of that passion.

In my consulting practice, I prefer the Extended DISC profile. It is also based on Carl Jung's behavioral science as well as the behavioral research conducted by early twentieth-century lawyer, inventor, and psychologist Dr. William Moulton Marston, creator of the first functioning lie-detector test. Thus, both MBTI and Extended DISC are adapted applications of Jung's theory. Extended DISC maintains a four-quadrant system (as opposed to the sixteen profiles in MBTI). This distinction makes it easier to learn and understand.

You and I know that we are all members of the same body and that each part has a role to play. But do you know your role? And do you truly embrace it? Do those around you know your role and value it? Our natural behavioral style is relevant in any situation: family, work, and volunteerism and servant leadership. So let's take a quick look at the DISC behavioral styles and see if you recognize your own.

Dominance. Do you stick with your decisions? Are you decisive, possessing the ability to move a room to action? If so, chances are you are a D style, and while some won't appreciate your decisiveness, your ability to review information and make an actionable decision is a benefit to your team. D styles can be described as direct, decisive, strong willed, and demanding.

Influence. Do you motivate those around you? If you have ever been told you are a cheerleader, chances are you an I style. Your outgoing, talkative nature inspires some but annoys others. How can your team keep playing without encouragers? I styles are described as spontaneous, talkative, enthusiastic, and persuasive.

Steadiness. Do you remain steady, even in crisis? Have you been known to wait patiently while people around you are in a tiff about waiting (huffing and puffing and making faces)? You could be an S style. Your laid-back nature provides a calming force to those around you, and that's not just needed when something is on fire—it's needed even before the logs are stacked! S styles are described as steady, calm, sincere, and stable.

Conscientiousness. Do you think critically and enjoy facts? Maybe you prefer to know all the significant digits in pi, while others are fine to round them. You likely fall into the C style category. C styles are described as precise, systematic, detailed, and logical. Your attention to detail can be an asset to your team, but your tendency to overthink things can slow you and your team down.

The reality is that while some of us have dominant styles that are clearly visible, we're all a combination of all four styles. Some of our behaviors are innate, and some have formed over time. I'm an engineer who loves people. In DISC I'm an I-C style or, as I put it, a fun, outgoing nerd.

Bear in mind you are not in a competition. Understanding how these roles work together is key. The eye can't say to the hand, "I don't need you." Knowing your natural behavioral style describes how you interact with others, and that information can provide insight into your interpersonal strengths. You may also find that you've learned to adapt your behaviors in certain situations but that your underlying preferences remain the same. For example, when I'm training or speaking, my I style takes over, and I ask my C style to take a back seat, but when I'm doing my taxes, it's the opposite.

How do you learn your dominant style to know which part you are naturally? The best way is to complete an Extended DISC questionnaire (for more information, visit the online resources). You can use the descriptions above to self-identify, but remember, the view you have of yourself needs to account for what others really see.

For a quick self-assessment, ask yourself two questions:

1. Are you task oriented or people oriented? They're both going to matter, but one is going to matter more. For some people it's pretty obvious, but for others it's not quite as obvious, so they may feel a little stuck in the middle. Choose which describes you best.

2. Are you reserved or active? Often this is a question of extroversion versus introversion, but not always. Just because people can stand up talking in front of a room doesn't mean they are extroverts. When they're done, they could be in the back, needing time to get over the whole situation because it took so much energy out of them. For me, interacting with people lights me up, and I'm energized for three or four more days. The answer to this question lies in where you derive your energy.

Plot your responses to these questions in the chart in your online companion resource and that will identify which quadrant—D, I, S, or C—that you think you best fit into. Compare this to the description of the styles above, and ask yourself, "Do I know my behavioral style?"

Natural Gifts and Talents

Now that you have reviewed your interpersonal strengths, you will also want to assess your natural gifts and talents. Natural gifts are innate, and talents are honed and developed over time. I love to use the example of my oldest son, Malcolm, who died in 2014 after battling cancer. He was a gifted artist. It was an innate gift given to him, and because he embraced that gift, he developed it into a talent, showcasing it and using it to decorate his and his brothers' rooms. Many people have gifts that they don't use, so they don't get seen as talents.

Take a spiritual gifts inventory. The source and type of gifts that a person possesses can differ based on a person's belief system. As a Christian, I view a certain set of gifts as spiritual gifts given to us by the Creator. According to theologians, there is no official list of spiritual gifts, but some commonly known ones are discernment (appraising a person or situation), evangelism (sharing the Gospel with others), exhortation (encouraging and strengthening others), faith, giving, leadership, and teaching. The process of nurturing spiritual growth involves being able to discern which of these gifts we possess and which ones we do not (my choir director helped me with this).

Leadership (the ability to lead and influence people), administration (the ability to manage tasks effectively), and teaching (or passing knowledge) are my three prevailing gifts. I've learned from personal experience that when we identify our gifts, implement them, and use them correctly, we become more effective servant leaders. As I identify that which God has instilled in me to promote his purpose, my ability to serve improves. Find your gifts, and establish how you can use them to improve your life and the lives of those around you.

You may gain valuable insight in knowing which gifts were planted in you from birth. The online companion resources give instructions on how to complete a spiritual gifts inventory. The online tool also displays a complete listing of spiritual gifts and their descriptions.

Ask yourself, "Are there gifts that I'm not using?"

Listen to what others say. This may go against what your mother told you in the fifth grade, but there is some merit to what trusted friends and colleagues have to say about you. The key is to find individuals whose feedback is useful. Pay attention to the compliments they pay you, and make note of the things they ask

you to do. When I began serving in my church, the responses leaders had to my interactions with youths helped me see that engag-
ing with children and teens is one of my strengths. When there is
a need for a spokesperson (for my family, a group, or an organization), I am often asked or appointed. Sure, this means opening
yourself up to criticism, but it also means uncovering things that
you may not have noticed about yourself. Now ask yourself, "What
am I good at doing?"

CHAPTER 2

Know Your Weaknesses

• • •

To get a balanced picture of who you are while defining your strengths, you also have to explore your weaknesses. You will come face-to-face with yourself in ways that may seem uncomfortable at first. Getting to know your weaknesses will cause you to take a serious look at your choices, your priorities, and the way you interact with others.

While discomfort is a good thing, harping on your weaknesses is not. It is good practice to leverage your strengths and plan to develop your weaknesses over time. When you overemphasize your weaknesses, you risk lowering your self-esteem. I urge you to discern which limitations to focus on and which you simply need to accept. This practice is not complacency. Rather, this practice will help you gain important perspective. There is a line between being self-aware and being self-conscious; the latter can hold you back.

As you identify your personal shortcomings, you will begin to notice development areas that need your attention. For example, you might think to yourself, "I need to be more patient," or "I have a hard time redirecting people who don't make their deadlines." Exercises like this encourage more self-awareness. Leaders who are more self-aware are better equipped to improve themselves, their families, and their organizations.

Just as I did with my strengths, my journey of self-discovery led me to a variety of resources for identifying my development areas. You can identify your areas for growth by understanding your behavioral style, looking within, asking those around you, and analyzing your skills.

Behavioral Style Assessment

The Extended DISC assessment that showed you your strengths will also outline your development areas and provide insight into how they may affect your leadership and relationships. As noted before, there are no good or bad styles, just different styles. Each style has strengths and weaknesses. Knowing your behavioral style will provide you with insight into behaviors you may have become comfortable with but actually limit your effectiveness. These are areas that require more energy for you to master, and because of that, you may have neglected to develop them.

In addition to areas that don't come naturally, many people overuse their strengths in high-stress situations, and that can reflect as a weakness. For example, D styles are described as competitive, and that trait likely drives them and their teams to succeed. But overusing that strength could put undue stress on others and can lead to poor sportsmanship.

In a team setting, it's important to note those around you who augment you. In other words, your weakness could be their strengths. For example, it is a good strategy for a manager who is creative and people focused (I style) to have a team member who is discerning with an attention to detail (S style).

Knowing your behavioral style will also help you understand how you make decisions, how others perceive you, and how you play on a team. These are important insights for leading change in your organization or at home.

We have to know those things that we don't prefer and those things that we may not feel that we excel in. What can you do about something that you're not that good at? Try to improve. Rather than saying, "I'm not good at that," try to get better. If your manager wants you to give a presentation, you can't respond, "I'm an S style. I don't do presentations." No, no, no. You need to do the presentation. Plan for some time to decompress afterward; chances are you'll need it, but you're going to do it, and you're probably going to do a great job, because as an S style, you're going to make sure that you convey all your thoughts. There is not a list of tasks to which you can say, "I can't do that because I'm a D (or I, S, or C)." That's not what it's used for. It's used to help you understand how you can get the best out of yourself each day and where you can find those areas to do even more. I don't know about you, but every year, that's what I want: to do even more.

Look in the Mirror

Despite the availability of assessments and tests that can identify your development areas, there is still no substitute for a long, hard look in the mirror. Unlike in the fairy tale *Snow White*, asking "Mirror, mirror, on the wall, who is the fairest of them all?" won't get you closer to self-awareness, but reflecting on your attitudes, behaviors, and interpersonal skills will. This quiet introspection is necessary for any leader and helps reveal not just your outward behaviors but also your values, motives, and character.

In his book *The 7 Habits of Highly Effective People*, Dr. Stephen R. Covey writes about the maturity continuum and its importance for personal effectiveness. He defines the continuum as a shift from dependence (I need you to take care of me), to independence (I can do it), and then ultimately to interdependence (we can do it). Many adults consider themselves accomplished when they arrive at independence (they are "#adulting"), but truly effective leaders strive for interdependence.

In order to move toward interdependence, you have to possess empathy, which is understanding someone else's perspective. As Dr. Covey says, "If you can't see and feel the emotions of others, then you'll have a hard time influencing or leading others effectively."

Empathy requires us to control our emotions and maintain awareness of how we handle those tough moments that spark reactions from us. It is a pillar of emotional intelligence (EQ), which many thought leaders deem to be even more important than your intelligence quotient (IQ). So grab that mirror, and ask what it sees in your heart. As it says in Matthew 12:34 (NKJV), "For out of the abundance of the heart the mouth speaks."

Participate in a 360°

I firmly believe that another great way to discover your strengths and development areas is to listen to what others say about you. Their feedback can either affirm or deny your own thoughts. Many organizations conduct 360° evaluations, which allow you to receive feedback from your manager as well as those you lead and manage. It provides you with a great all-around picture of your effectiveness in certain areas. I recognized a long time ago that my leanings toward speaking stemmed from listening to others who enjoyed hearing me speak and who urged me to pursue it professionally. Although I could have just run with it, I knew I had to spend time further developing my speaking skills. The feedback affirmed my gift, but I knew it was up to me to develop it.

Beyond affirming a gift that needs to be developed, effective feedback can help identify skills that need to be learned. For example, I received input from an associate that I wasn't a good listener—ouch! I rushed to purchase Michael Nichols's *The Lost Art of Listening* so that I could develop my listening skills. As an I style, I tend to do my best thinking when someone else is talking, and I have to be intentional not to do that.

I love using the example of muscles because I'm a runner. I can still hear my track coach telling me, "Georgia"—he liked to call me Georgia because my name is pronounced "Atlanta" without the *t*'s—"you've got to work on your abs because when you lift your legs, you've got to have strong abs. You can have strong quads. But if you have weak abs, you're not going to run a good four-hundred-meter dash." I was competitive, and I wanted to run a strong four hundred meters. So what do you think I did? Yep, I started working on my abs.

A University of California, Los Angeles, study revealed that people remember 70 percent of the negative things they hear. When you receive feedback, keep that in mind. Balance out the input, and keep a healthy perspective on the criticism and praise. In addition to that, I typically skim off the most positive and the most negative comments I receive because the truth often lies somewhere in the middle.

Skills Gap Assessment

As you assess your abilities beyond your interpersonal skills, you may want to consider doing a skills gap analysis. This simple technique requires you to list the skills you need for a role and examine your current level of understanding of each required skill. For example, developing organizational skills to progress in your career will also help you become more organized at home.

The online companion resources have a table with skills for project managers. If you are filling (or aspiring to fill) a different role, enter the skills required for that position. If you're unsure what skills are required for a position, reach out to your Human Resources/Talent Development department or search online for "skills required for _____."

Skills are not usually a "yes or no" question (do you have them or not) but rather a "what level do you possess" question. For that reason, your skills assessment should use a scale of one through five, with one being limited or no knowledge and five indicating expertise or mastery. The skills on the higher end of the scale are your strengths, and those on the lower end should help you identify where to focus your development efforts. Fulfillment is found in opportunities to leverage your skills.

Left ignored, weak areas can keep you from moving forward, so don't run from them. Instead, identify them, and make positive changes that will help you become a better individual and leader. It should not be your goal to excel in every area, so be sure to praise progress. Ask yourself, "What development areas should I focus on?"

CHAPTER 3

Know Your Motivations

• • •

Your motivations are an important part of self-exploration—of understanding what motivates you to do what you do. We all have intrinsic motivators. Those are the things that no one has to ask you to do. You just want to do them, and you do a great job as long as you continue to work hard. Some of the things we are motivated to do aren't necessarily talents, but they can develop into talents because we are driven to do them.

Intrinsic motivation is simply that which motivates us because it's who we are. Everyone has intrinsic motivation, just not for the same things. It's not a correct statement to say that you're not motivated unless there is an action associated with it. In other words, you may not be motivated to do your taxes, but you may be motivated to go for a walk. People who are intrinsically motivated aren't seeking reward or recognition for that action. We feel that internal tug at our heartstrings and act upon it. People often ask me how I made the leap from petroleum engineering and IT (highly technical) to leadership and team performance (highly people focused), and the answer lies in getting to truly know myself. The more I explored my strengths and my motivations, the more I moved from petroleum science and processes to behavioral science and performance. People and science fascinate me!

I spent my entire personal life navigating change, figuring out how to overcome obstacles, and pushing through adversity. I've spent my professional life teaching others how to do the same. I found that there was a purpose behind the pain that I experienced in my youth. I found that there was a reason for every situation, for every lesson, and for every time that I had to try harder and push harder in order to succeed. I was motivated to share my story in my books and public speaking to encourage others. If you haven't been motivated to write a book, it doesn't mean you aren't motivated; it means you are motivated in other ways, and you owe it to yourself to figure out what they are.

Your Passions and Interests

In my *What's Your Catalyst? The Power of Managed Change* workshops, I open with an activity encouraging participants to share their answers to two questions: where are two of your favorite destinations, and where is one place you want to go?

The outcome is always the same: I can't get the room to settle down! For some facilitators, this would be frightening, but it always makes my point that people will go on and on about what they are passionate about. The answers aren't always "Because they have great beaches." I often hear things like "That's where my grandchildren live, and they mean the world to me."

So, think about your answers. If you were in a room with someone, would you go on and on about the destinations you chose and the why behind them? The answer is likely yes because people love to talk about things that interest them. Now consider this: if someone asked you what you do for work, would you go on and on? If that answer is "not lately," then you need to do a passion check and reconnect with the reason you chose your profession or look at adjustments you can make to infuse more passion into your workplace.

What we're passionate about moves us, and what moves us motivates us. But in order for our passions to positively impact our lives, we have to identify them. Ask yourself, "What do I love to do?" Because love is a catalyst.

My passion for traveling (and my talent for planning) moved me to open a home-based travel agency shortly after my return from Africa. It wasn't until after I left the company that I realized this "hobby business" could be the start of a new season for me. Starting that business translated into my ability to serve people, learn to run a business, and travel with my family at a discount. It's great when our passions open doors!

Behavioral Style Assessment

Consider your motivations. What makes you want to go to work each day? What makes you tick? The Extended DISC assessment reveals a list of motivators that help you realize your comfort zones and how you can leverage them. For example, I like to work with happy people, so I am often the social coordinator on a team, looking for ways to encourage togetherness.

Just as your behavioral style will point out your motivators, you can also find out what demotivates you. Do deadlines and pressure motivate you or shut you down? What about conflict? Different styles respond to these situations differently. When you know your behavioral style, you gain insight into what lights you up and brings out the best in you and what diminishes your shine.

Values and Priorities

When it all comes down to it, our values drive our priorities. Your values are what matter most to you, and you hold them near, seldom willing to look away. I mentioned that during my trip to Africa, the time away from my family was difficult. The trip revealed that what I held dearest to me was not getting the majority of my time.

I felt compelled to adjust my work schedule. What I valued most was time with my children.

Your values are introduced to you by your family of origin, but they can morph over time. They can provide a spiritual and emotional direction for you. They are a function of the experiences you've had, and they can motivate you to pursue certain goals, hinder you from pursuing others, and cause you to draw certain conclusions.

Take Richard, who attended one of my workshops. He came from a large family and looked at Sundays as an opportune time to visit his aging mother and his siblings. When approached with career opportunities that would require him to relocate, he declined them in favor of staying close to his family, even if that meant limiting his options.

Compelling Reasons

Often, people are motivated extrinsically by *why* they do something more so than by *what* they do. There's a *why* behind everything we do. This becomes a key component to personal change. When leaders implement change within organizations, they must tell people why the change is occurring and help them connect the change to a purpose. As change leaders in our organizations and change leaders in ourselves, we have to constantly ask why.

If a change is needed, you must figure out the reason for—the motivation behind—the necessary change. You have to ask yourself what positive impact the change will bring and examine the consequences for not making the change. You might ask yourself, "If I don't do this, what will happen?"

Most of us at some point have wanted to lose weight, and there has always been a *why*, be it a health reason or a vanity reason. Vanity is a great motivator, and I don't knock people for having it; sometimes that's what keeps us making healthy choices. Knowing that summer is coming packs people into gyms. You want to craft statements that remind you of your personal reasons. The impact statement that drives personal and professional change is, If I don't do x by z, then what will happen? Years ago, I got on the scale and realized that if I didn't lose forty pounds in six to seven months, I would increase my risk of getting diabetes or other health issues. I knew my family medical history predisposed me to certain conditions, and I didn't want to increase my likelihood of developing those conditions. That was my *why*. Starting a fitness regimen was my *what*, and my *why* has allowed me to maintain it. Your catalyst is critical to creating and maintaining change in your life.

Think about something that you want to change. It could be a big change or a small one. Write it down. Ask yourself, "If I don't do x by y, what will happen?" As you put the pieces together to understand your catalyst for change in a particular area of your life, you will see that it is tied to your motivators. What's the consequence if you don't get your certification? Do you have one?

Likewise, if you're trying to modify something in your organization, an effective way to get people to adopt change is making sure they understand what will happen if they don't. What's the implication if they don't change? Ask yourself, "What am I eager to do?"

CHAPTER 4

Know Your Life Lessons

$$\bullet \ \bullet \ \bullet$$

One of a project manager's most useful tools is a "lessons learned" register, which is a list of project challenges and successes that serve as knowledge for future projects. Project professionals who use this tool wisely learn to convert the knowledge into wisdom by heeding the warnings contained within it. As stated in Proverbs 13:20, "Walk with the wise and become wise, for the companion of fools suffers harm."

A true knowledge-management champion understands the value of capturing these lessons learned as we go along on our projects, as opposed to waiting until the end. One way to do this is by journaling your present life experiences so that you have the details and insight you need to truly learn from the past.

Just like on projects, you can learn a lot about yourself when you explore your past. In my memoir, *Love Is a Catalyst: The Pain behind the Purpose*, I share an assignment I give my coaching clients: chronicle your highs and lows to gain a balanced perspective of your life story. You don't have to share them, but I do encourage you to write them down. Now that you have started this journal, you can commit to maintaining it for your future life reviews.

My personal assignment revealed a desire to be more present and engaged with my children than my parents were with me. My father had to work a lot (very common in working-class families), while my mom, who also worked full time, struggled to overcome her childhood wounds and suffered great harm as a result. Expanding my analysis to the next generation also revealed patterns that I wanted to break. For instance, my maternal grandmother never told me, "I love you."

When you take a close look at the events and people that have shaped your life, you gain keen insight into patterns and preferences that could impact your future. While exploring your closet of life experiences, remember that it's not just the event that's important to note but what you learned from it. Your *always* may have formed because it was someone's *never*.

Replay Your Story

One way to perform this self-analysis is to play a game, which I call the "Game of Life." In this activity, you divide your life so far into four quarters (like a football game): childhood, adolescence, young adulthood, and adulthood (to the present day). Each quarter can range from ten to twelve years, and the quarters don't have to be equal. Feel free to use a different time frame if you want. Make it yours. The idea is to look back and consider your past. Once you've broken down the quarters, you can begin to roll the game footage and look for themes or patterns.

For example, early childhood is the first quarter. Early twenties could be your second quarter. Your third quarter could be your thirties, and your fourth quarter is the season that you are in now. You can take where you are right now and divide it by four. They don't have to be equal, so you C styles can put your calculators away! The whole point of knowing yourself and your life lessons is knowing your story. Think of how your story impacts you. When you look at your behavioral style, you know that's what you were born with. Now you can see how your story, your behavioral styles, and your motivations connect. You can learn from the past. Remember, in the "Game of Life," you don't lose, you learn!

In my memoir, I talk about the chaotic changes I endured throughout my life. For example, I moved so much as a child that by the time I entered seventh grade, I had attended eleven different schools, including three different schools in one year! As a result, I didn't have the opportunity to maintain relationships, not even with family. I was no stranger to change.

Today I look back on all those moves and realize every change taught me how to meet new people and adapt to new environments. Moving also taught me to value time with my extended family because I didn't have enough of it as a child.

I survived a turbulent upbringing. Even so, my childhood taught me how to brave the rapids. In my "Game of Life," those movements marked my first-quarter lows and highs. My childhood was chilly.

My adolescent and teen years proved to be even more challenging after my once-present mother became addicted to crack cocaine and abandoned me. Moving suddenly from Seattle back to Houston in seventh grade with a few belongings in a duffle bag caused a deep erosion in my self-esteem. I only saw my mom sporadically for years, adding to my feelings of abandonment. Thankfully I was able to live with my father, and even when times were hard, I never went without a place to stay.

But it got worse. My mother was murdered at the start of my senior year in high school. I reacted by brushing away the tears and pushing my way through to college with an academic scholarship. High school marks the end of my second quarter, a stormy time that I have to think long and hard to find a high in. While writing my memoir, I was able to find it. I had amazing high school track coaches who instilled in me a love for running that is still with me to this day, and I had a father who raised a wounded teenage girl all by himself.

Although my second quarter was marked with pain, my biggest mistake was not allowing myself time to grieve. As a result, I struggled during my first semester in college. The hole that I dug was too deep, and I lost my scholarship. I worked my way through school and received my petroleum-engineering degree in 1995.

In 1999, as I was ending my first marriage (which only lasted three years), it all hit me like a ton of bricks. When I remarried a year later, I became an instant mom to three beautiful boys, but I had a wounded heart and a stressful career in oil and gas. I was barely holding it together, and I knew I had to do better. In addition, I had a series of deaths in the family. The combination of abandonment issues, grief, and stress had been taking its toll on me on the inside. Most people couldn't tell on the outside because I had it all tucked away in my life "closet," a survival technique I learned in my childhood. One day in 2006, I retreated to my "closet," where I had an emotional breakdown. After that, I challenged myself daily to become a better leader at home and at work. I recommitted to my faith and began the process of healing, which started with cleaning out my "closet."

It all sounds so melodramatic, yet as I analyze each major event, I can see how each one helped shape me. I see the benefits of the resilience and self-reliance that I gained from my trials. Still, I had to acknowledge that I was struggling with my faith and the compassion that it teaches. My self-reliance was both a blessing and a curse. I needed to be self-sufficient, yet God reliant. Roses are beautiful, resilient plants that protect themselves with thorns. Spiritually and emotionally, I needed to reduce my thorns. That is the theme for my fourth quarter: trimming the thorns.

Review Your Career History

Professionally, I saw a similar pattern. I started my career in the remote south Texas field operations and endured brutal conditions, abusive people, and isolation for almost two years (the result of being the only woman on an all-male crew). I was the only woman in the field for miles, and my twenty-four-hour on-call work schedule didn't allow for much of a social life. Thus, because of where I was spiritually and emotionally, I just couldn't handle my job any longer. The day I was about to quit, I received word that I was being transferred from small-town Alice, Texas, to suburban Sugar Land, just outside of Houston. This would give me a normal work schedule and would move me closer to family.

I moved immediately and started an exciting career in IT. I went from depressed and shut down to instantly eager to contribute. I did what hadn't been done (or even attempted) before and learned to write code and install databases to keep pace with our quickly moving SAP invoicing and logistics system rollout. I then proudly launched systems that improved the efficiency of the oil-field services giant all over the world! I worked long hours, and I traveled extensively, training and conducting meetings on every continent except Australia and Antarctica (and Africa, which had still eluded me at that point). Just as in life, I became a champion of change in my organization, and I thrived on using project management to do it.

My first project was intended to bring about a massive amount of disruption to an industry that didn't particularly like change. I recall being mentored by technicians who kept their best information in tally books in their back pockets. They would jot down notes and capture data that they would reference on their next job. They would also use this information to know what happened at the wellsite and what to charge the clients. The undertaking I embarked on was going to digitize and standardize invoicing and data capture for the entire company. First, however, people had to be taught how to do things the "new way." Armed with the authority of upper management, I was prepared to bullishly get people to put away their notepads and old ways of doing things and quickly adopt this new way. Boy, was I in for a lesson (or two). Here are a few of my favorites.

For many, change feels like a loss. When you ask people to make a large-scale change like I was, you have to be prepared for them to grieve the loss of their current situations. While writing things down in a book seemed trivial to me, the comfort and control that people had grown accustomed to were in jeopardy, and as with any emotional loss, I didn't have to fully understand it to help them through it. I needed only to acknowledge the depth of their feelings and go from there.

"You catch more flies with honey than with vinegar." This old adage holds especially true when trying to bring about change. Finding kind ways to get people to adapt to change is just as essential as politely asking the toddler to put the toys away. Pounding your fist on a desk may get someone to appear to agree with you, but you won't see the results in the long run. When adopting change, it's not the short-term appearance that matters; it's the sustaining of the new state that will allow you to declare victory.

I'm a quick study. So, before I realized it, I found myself telling people that "it would all be OK" right in the middle of the training. Setting their minds at ease and even just listening to their concerns went a long way in helping them take the necessary new steps and replace their tally books with laptops. That lesson helped me learn how to help people adapt to change. It was also one I would have to say to myself repeatedly in my own development.

I also realized from charting my career highs and lows that I was the most excited about a project in the beginning, when I was working with stakeholders to gather requirements and, toward the end, when I had the opportunity to teach and inspire them to adopt the change in front of them.

I was an engineer-turned-IT professional who loved helping people. Armed with this information, I moved into the Talent Development Department in 2000 to direct IT. I also helped with recruiting, retaining, and training engineers and technicians all over the world. My career path began to deviate from what I was passionate about. In 2005, the trip to Africa put it all into perspective.

I loved helping people learn and grow, and I wanted that to be the focus of my career.

You don't have to write or publish a memoir to reflect on your own life lessons, but I encourage you to put pen to paper and reflect on the pivotal moments in your life. They will reveal a lot about your purpose and will help you uncover your passions. Refer to the online resources for guidelines on how you can create an outline of your life lessons and map out your highs and lows. Do this for personal events, and take a look at your career history. It is a proven fact that discontent in one area will spill over into the other, so be sure to review your personal and professional life lessons together.

What you see is not about you. The lessons that you've learned and the challenges that you've faced are not about you. As you grow in your leadership, you will have opportunities to impact others. Let that become your personal mantra: it's not about me!

CHAPTER 5

Know Your Unique Purpose

• • •

The in-depth study of yourself reveals the most important thing about you: your unique purpose. Like a fingerprint, your purpose is unique to you and unlike anyone else's. It establishes the vision for your life and differentiates your path from others'. Everything on earth has a purpose, a reason for existing, and a role in the grand scheme. That purpose is unique to it. Take ships for example. While on my trip to West Africa in 2005, I had a chance to tour a stimulation treatment vessel called the *Galaxie*. This monstrous ship was engineered to provide hydraulic-fracture treatments, also known as fracking, to offshore wells. The ship had sleeping quarters for the crew, supplies to meet their needs, and technology to service the wells. These high-tech treatment ships weren't pretty, but they certainly served a purpose: improved reservoir production, which is very important in oil and gas.

Interestingly, just a month after that trip, I went on my first cruise to celebrate my uncle Lurie's birthday. We boarded a massive cruise ship in Galveston, Texas, that was engineered for fun. The ship, named the *Carnival Ecstasy*, had sleeping quarters for the crew and dining and entertainment for its guests. There was a pool, a casino, and a basketball court for recreation. It was similar to the *Galaxie* that I toured in the offshore oil-field waters. But it had a different purpose, which was to entertain and bring delight to its guests. For five days, it did just that! Like the ships that sail the seven seas, we are all engineered for purpose.

After I returned from Africa, I asked myself, "Am I walking in my purpose?" I wondered if I was using my gifts and my strengths to impact the world.

My heart said, Sometimes.

I knew that wasn't enough. I wanted to establish a life that demonstrated my purpose and leveraged my position consistently. My career was important to me, and just prior to departing for the trip, I achieved my Project Management Professional (PMP) certification. This marked a career milestone for me, one that could lead me to further elevation in the company and the credentials I needed to be a consultant. I was already a leader in my industry, but my soul-searching revealed that I wanted to be a better leader at home and in my community. I had accomplished an important goal, and I asked myself, "Now what?"

"For Such a Time as This"

The Old Testament story of Esther describes the plight of a young Jewish woman who was put in a position to help save her people from destruction. She had gained the ear of the king and, as such, could request that he change the plan he had to destroy the Israelites. There was one problem: confronting the king would cost her dearly; it could even cost her life. She was reminded by her cousin that she was in a powerful position, and he caused her to consider whether she had been put in that position "for such a time as this" (Esther 4:14).

While I wasn't empowered to single-handedly save a community from destruction, I was sure my trip to Africa was no accident and that my actions had a tremendous positive impact on the lives of others. The story of Esther reminded me that I should be on the lookout for other such times that highlight my purpose.

On August 29, 2005, Hurricane Katrina hit the US Gulf Coast. When it hit, Rodney and I happened to be sitting in a Las Vegas airport awaiting our flight back to our home in Houston. We were in Las Vegas vacationing with friends who had family members who lived in New Orleans. We all watched from the airport's television monitors as Katrina approached Louisiana with cyclonic force. When we boarded the plane, New Orleans had received the all clear. The hurricane had dumped rain, but all seemed well.

However, it wasn't until we landed that we learned about the levee break in New Orleans's Ninth Ward and the subsequent destruction that was caused. We learned that our friend's family lost everything. Impacted by what I had witnessed just four months earlier in West Africa, I knew that I had to take action. I could not simply do nothing knowing that, like the cholera outbreak that could have been eradicated but wasn't because of complacency or heartlessness, I could make a difference and impact lives.

I was limited in what I could do because I had to work. Nonetheless, I refused to simply watch and listen. For a moment, I felt helpless, thinking there was nothing I could do. Then I recalled my uncle's "Or is there?" It was in incredible opportunity to show love and grace to those who needed it most, and I didn't want to miss it. So, in the evenings, I volunteered at a local church helping people who arrived ahead of the storm. It turned out they needed volunteers to assist with computers and help people apply for jobs since they now had nothing to return to.

The situation worsened, and they set up a temporary shelter in the Astrodome, which is about forty minutes from my home. I took a couple of days of unscheduled vacation time so I could volunteer. I had no idea what to expect. My only point of reference was what I saw on television. None of that mattered, however; I just wanted to help. Immediately after I walked into the colossal dome, I heard moans of pain and sobbing in the distance, just as the broadcasters had described. Between watching children in Malabo drink dirty, diseased water to now witnessing the wailing of mothers, children, the elderly, and entire families who had to flee for their lives with just the clothes on their backs, my heart broke.

I was assigned to help distribute snacks and hand sanitizer. Without even realizing it, I began praying for a grieving woman who had lost her child to the floodwaters. After I prayed, I instinctively entertained her other two children. Dirty water caused devastation again, but this time here at home in the United States.

After my trip to Africa and after serving the victims of Hurricane Katrina, I was gaining confidence in my purpose. I wanted to be more of a servant leader both at home and at work. I wanted to be more charitable with my time, talents, and treasures. To do that, I needed to start my own business and set my own work schedule.

My motivation this time, however, was different. I recognized clear overlaps in my professional and personal priorities. One of the reasons why I wanted to start my own consulting businesses was because I wanted to have autonomy over the projects I led. Personally, after the jarring and eye-opening occurrences (the naked boy carrying diseased water, mothers watching their babies die on a hot bridge in New Orleans, and more), I saw entrepreneurship as a way to do what I was called to do. That is my *why*—my catalyst. It spells out my purpose and is fueled by my passion. And, because purpose and position go hand in hand, I wanted to impact my family and the world while still having a successful career. Esther's story became more real to me.

I took a deep breath, and I began to pray about my purpose. I sought direction about what I was being called to do and how to begin moving forward. I knew that I was born to do this.

I had four beautiful boys to raise with the challenges of a blended family. I saw, from my own unstable childhood, that I wanted to provide them with a firm foundation of love and a legacy of faith. In addition to that, I felt a strong call to teach and inspire others from my life experiences, both personally and professionally. I found meaning in the proverbial statement "As iron sharpens iron, so one man sharpens another," and it became my theme. I knew that I was engineered for purpose.

I was then able to translate that theme into a personal mission statement: to grow in wisdom and to inspire leaders who are encouraged by their faith, provide for their families, and impact the world. This statement took years of refinement and guides me in my decisions, at work and at home

Now You Know Your Why

Your unique purpose is the reason why you are here; it's what you were designed for. It will define who you are, drive what you do, and determine the contributions you make to the world. It may prompt you to do things completely differently, or it may encourage you to achieve smaller, incremental improvements in your being. As you navigate the stages of growth in your life, knowing your purpose will help you create the vision statement that you need to effectively implement and sustain change in your life. It will help you "run with perseverance the race set out for you" (Heb. 12:1). Ask yourself, "Am I doing what I was engineered to do? Am I living out my purpose?"

Knowing yourself means taking the mirror you used to evaluate your skills and holding it over your heart. Doing so will reveal what is deeply rooted and established in you and help reveal your purpose, passions, and priorities. Collectively they define your *why*, and now you know your catalyst.

PART 2

Make a Strategic Plan

• • •

The plans of the diligent lead to profit as surely as haste leads to poverty.

—Proverbs 21:5

Now that you know who you are and you understand your *why*— your catalyst—you're ready to take action. But wait! Don't just make moves; make strategic moves!

To transition from where you are to where you want to be, you need a strategic plan—a road map that ties to your purpose. First, you need to understand strategic change leadership. Then follow these steps:

- Step 1: Decide

- Step 2: Devise

- Step 3: Do

- Step 4: Review

CHAPTER 6

Understand Strategic Change Leadership

• • •

Now that you understand where you are—your strengths, weaknesses, motivations, lessons, and purpose—you can begin the process of identifying where you want to be. As you journeyed through self-discovery in Part 1, "Know Yourself," you likely found areas in your life that you want to improve or change, but don't get ahead of yourself. As you plan to grow and adapt, you want to be true to your authentic self. You began to create a vision for your future. Strategic planning is about creating a road map of how to make that vision a reality. It's about ordering your steps to get to your future state. Use strategic change leadership to get you there.

Conducting a thorough SWOT (strengths, weaknesses, opportunities, and threats) analysis will help you in the formation of your strategic plan and help you identify any barriers to your progress. Your strengths and weaknesses were evaluated in Part 1. You now need to look externally to find opportunities to maximize and threats to minimize on your path to success. Your online companion resource has more details and a worksheet to help you conduct a SWOT analysis for your career and personal strategy.

What Do You See?

Strategic planning starts with a vision. It is a high-level understanding of who you want to be, the contributions you want to make, and the legacy you want to leave. Ask yourself, "What is my vision for my life?" Strategic growth planning involves thinking realistically about your long-term goals, looking ahead and imagining your success, and ensuring that your purpose is fulfilled. Financial planners do this for retirement and beyond. It is essential to have not only a financial plan for the future stages of life but also a legacy plan. When I'm nearing my twilight, I want to have meaningful relationships and a list of accomplishments and be financially secure.

As I began to look ahead, I pictured the impact I would make in the lives of others. I reaffirmed my purpose, "to sharpen iron," and I allowed that to guide my life choices (my children were the most important "iron"). I found myself reading the bios and obituaries of people I admired, thinking about what key contributions I would want included in my own when the time came.

I saw the vision for my career taking shape based on my priorities. I envisioned that the next ten to fifteen years would have a greater emphasis on being a work-from-home mom and that as my children grew older and more independent, I could deliver more in-person training. Teaching is my passion, so I would conduct it virtually for a season and then transition. My long-term vision was to continue teaching all over the world, continuing my quest to teach on every continent. This would allow me to fulfill my purpose of helping people grow.

We often think about where we want to live, how long we will work, and what types of activities we'll participate in. Depending on your age and stage of life, your strategic plan may involve looking five to ten years into the future. What do you see as your role in the workplace and at home in five years? In ten years? In fifteen years? Ask yourself, "What kind of legacy do I want to leave at work and at home?"

When the Vision Is Unclear

As I began to think about the legacy I wanted to leave, I began to see an even longer-term vision than my original fifteen-year plan. Looking this far into the future felt uncomfortable, especially given that my mother was only thirty-nine when she died. I realized I had a hard time imagining the future, and that realization opened my eyes to an important area of ministry I would serve in: helping people overcome grief and loss to see a bright future ahead.

If your life or career plan is unclear, spend time in prayer or meditate on what you want your vision to be. Ask for wisdom, and you will get it. Seek wise counsel to help clear roadblocks in your thinking, and refer to experts around you with visionary insights. If you find yourself unable to move forward, you are likely trapped in "paralysis by analysis," and you should look for guidance instead of going it alone.

Still stuck? Still uncertain? That's OK; move anyway. Sometimes to get clarity on your vision you have to start taking small steps and continually evaluate how they fit into the big picture. I mentioned that my passions led me to start a home-based travel business. That same venture allowed me to move *while* I sought clarity. Sometimes this feasibility study gives you information you can use to continue in a direction or to change directions altogether. Ultimately, your trial runs (if properly evaluated) can help inform the long-term decisions you make. I'm not encouraging you to move haphazardly; your feasibility steps should be low-investment actions that help you evaluate your long-term vision.

Before making plans, I usually like to have clarity. I strive for a clear understanding of the full situation and look for any obstacles that I may encounter. That clarity gives me confidence. However, life has taught me that it's not always possible to see everything. As a result, I have learned to trust God with my plans and to seek him daily instead of worrying. I began to see things turn out for my good even though they were confusing to my analytical mind (my C style really kicks in for planning).

When I made the decision to leave the comfort of the company that recruited me out of college, I did so on wobbly knees. It's a mistake to think that stepping out in faith looks like a fearless warrior soldier ready for battle. It often looks like a frightened child moving *anyway*. And because of the fear that I had (more on that later), I started in one direction while I gathered up the courage to really pursue my goal of starting my own business.

How Do You Get There?

Whether you are a project professional, an operations manager, or the family vacation planner, chances are you have the essential skill set for both project and change management. Project management involves the set of processes that allow you to accomplish project objectives. Change management is a systematic approach to managing and implementing change (often across an entire organization). In a professional setting, the methodologies complement each other to create, implement, and sustain change according to a strategic plan that is in place.

It is this strategic plan that must be considered first, and it is often overlooked. Your vision (who you want to be in the future) leads to your mission (what you are doing to get there), which leads to your strategic imperatives (the must-do goals you set). Your strategic plan for life encompasses your vision, mission, and goals. As you evaluate your vision and what matters most to you, your goals will reflect your purpose, passion, and priorities.

To realize your vision, you need to systematically take action to achieve your goals. Remember, you are the owner of your life, so you cast the vision. As long as your goals are aligned with that vision, your plans will succeed more often, and you will have a greater sense of fulfillment. To achieve that sense of fulfillment, you need strategic project management.

Is It a Project?

We all know and love that line from William Shakespeare's *Romeo and Juliet* warning us that a name does not define a person: "A rose by any other name would smell as sweet." So why do people go through so much trouble to take the word *project* and turn it into *initiative*? Don't get me wrong, *initiative* does sound a bit more intriguing, but why has the word *project* become a bad word? I've even been guilty of saying, "I don't want to turn this into a project," when referring to something simple that I am somehow making complicated with the use of my word choice. The accepted notion (even to me as a project manager) is that projects are big. They take a long time and require lots of people, planning, and resources. And initiatives are, well, different.

But the reality is that projects come in lots of sizes and lengths, just like roses come in different colors and varietals. If it passes the litmus test of being a "temporary endeavor undertaken to create a unique product, service, or result" (*PMBoK* 6th Ed., 2017), then it's a project, whether you want to call it that or not and whether it took you one month or one year to complete. Projects by their very nature create change, so whether you call the goals in your life projects or initiatives, to succeed you still have to manage them like a project.

To simplify the process of planning and executing the projects (or initiatives) that tie to your personal and professional vision, I've developed an easy Four-Step Strategic Change Leadership model: Decide, Devise, Do, and Review. This framework will guide you go in leading change...the Ms. Engineer Way. The subsequent chapters will explain how to use the strategies in this model for your personal and professional growth and development.

CHAPTER 7

Decide Your Goals

• • •

All action begins with a decision: a clear *what*, based on an understood *why*. In the project-management world, this is known as the "business case," or project justification. There has to be a clear reason to embark on a project or initiative and an awareness of the specific benefits that will arise from the change. A benefits analysis is done up front to confirm that the effort will be worth it. The project gets broadly defined, and the problem you want to solve gets clearer. The question is then asked, "Does this align with our business strategy?" The answers are defined up front and communicated often.

When I would pitch a project in my organization that needed funding, I would start with the business case and identify how the project would impact the organization. It had to have some benefit to the company, ideally financial, because if it doesn't make dollars, it doesn't make sense. For example, I implemented a new learning management system (LMS) not only because it would help people but also because it would allow managers and employees to direct their training, improve competency, and reduce costs in the training department. I also knew that when employees are empowered to manage their development, they succeed more often.

In regard to your personal life, this strategy involves seeking clarity about why you need a goal. In other words, how will it benefit you? This ensures that your goals are strategic and not arbitrary. Remember, not all change, in business or in life, is good change. Ask yourself, "Does this align with the vision I have for my life?"

When I decided to start my own business, I knew my reasons why: to have time to grow spiritually, time to raise my children, and time to serve my community. I wanted to have a life of significance, servant leadership, and excellence and then ultimately help people to be leaders of purpose and significance.

This was my business case, my catalyst, my *why*. When I decided to live a consistently active lifestyle and resume running (a goal that aligned with my vision), I knew that, given my family's history of diabetes, my life depended on it. I also knew that to make the kind of impact that I desired in my family and community, I needed to be healthy and have energy. That was my *why*. In both cases, the initiative I launched tied into my vision and purpose for my life.

You may relate to my reasons, or you may have a completely different set of your own. As you prioritize what needs to change first, create a strategy to accomplish your goals. Too often leaders jump right in and begin to devise. They are eager to create a plan and work through the processes that break down how much work needs to be done. Yet, in their zeal, they often overlook the Decide stage. They forget to align their goals with their organization's long-term strategic goals and underestimate the effort that it will take. In life, the same thing occurs. Individuals eager to change something may think through the steps, reminding themselves of what great planners they are (as evidenced by great family vacation pictures), but without a compelling business case (their catalyst), their plan won't succeed.

Is This the Season?

The book of Ecclesiastes provides timeless wisdom and insight, and in verse 3:18, King Solomon writes, "To everything there is a season, and a time to every purpose under the heaven" (NKJV). In a corporate portfolio, the decision to embark on a project is weighed against the organization's vision, mission, and values. Projects are lined up and prioritized to see which ones need to be completed first, second, and so on. This method of project selection asks the question, "Of all the projects we think are right (have a solid *why*), is this the one we should do right now?"

Throughout our lives, we have continual conversations with ourselves about what our passions, purpose, and priorities are. When we ask, "What can I do?" we may get slightly different answers each time. That's because situations change depending on the season. Situations don't change like the weather in Houston, which fluctuates from hot to cold and back to hot in one week, but they change over time—there are seasonal changes that occur throughout our lives.

Before I had children, my career was my top priority. But after I got married in 2000 and was instantly gifted with three handsome boys to pour into, my priorities changed. And then when I had a baby in 2003 (my fourth boy), my priorities shifted again. Life is constantly changing, so asking yourself, "Is this the season?" is the best way to ensure that the change you want is the change you need, when you need it. You may find yourself eager to explore a new business venture, go back to school for an advanced degree, or push for a new position or project with extra responsibilities. Remember to check the weather and see if it's the season for you.

What Does Success Look Like?

A well-written goal includes criteria that determine what is considered success. And since success is a journey, a strategic growth plan should include measurements for both the short term (achieving the goal) and the long term (maintaining the goal).

One place where this is evident is in health and nutrition. What every diet plan has in common is the requirement to pay close attention to what you're eating while also monitoring what you're doing. You see this in commercials about counting calories, food points, or carbs. To improve your health, you have to change your lifestyle, and that requires a change in input (foods you eat) and output (activity and exercise).

Studies have shown that the formula for most adults to achieve weight loss follows a 70:30 ratio: 70 percent input and 30 percent output. According to that formula, what you eat is more important. When I decided to improve my health by running, I knew I had to monitor my miles and my meals. You can't change what you don't measure.

Now it's your turn to assess your own decisions. Select three goals that align with your purpose, passion, and priorities. Fill in the blanks:

1. I've decided to _____ because _____ will happen. The best time to do this is _____.

2. I've decided to _____ because _____ will happen. The best time to do this is _____.

3. I've decided to _____ because _____ will happen. The best time to do this is _____.

Once you have clarity on why you want to change (your catalyst) and what you want to change (your goals), you can then move to the next step, which is Devise.

CHAPTER 8

Devise a Strategic Plan

• • •

You need to carefully devise a plan that will take into account the responses to your internal (and external) questions. Winston Churchill said, "The plan is nothing, but planning is everything." With so many things happening in your life beyond your control, the ability to plan includes the need to be proactive (thinking ahead) and adaptive (responding to change). The combination will allow you to create a plan for life that accounts for life!

For an analytical, critical thinker, this is likely the best part. Devising a plan to accomplish a strategic objective involves more than just laying out steps; it requires thinking about several parts. It's like sitting down to start a chess game and thinking several moves ahead. Creating an effective plan requires attention to detail, but it also requires a high-level, vision-minded perspective.

In my project-management workshops, I remind my students of the old joke "How do you eat an elephant?"

The answer is "one bite at a time."

Planning for a business or personal initiative is the exact same thing. It is defining the work that needs to be done and the effort that a team has to put into something in order to make it come to pass. When creating a plan to manage your life and career, there are limiting factors (or constraints) that have to be taken into account along with your own contributions. For example, pursuing a certification or advanced degree requires a time and money commitment that has to be sustained.

To help you understand how these constraints work together, try this quick exercise: Close your eyes and visualize in your mind a triangle. Each side has a different label. *Scope* is on the bottom, and *time* and *cost* are on the other sides. In project management, this labeled triangle is known as the "Triple Constraint" because it shows the relationship between the three most important constraints (scope, time, and cost) of a project. Any modifications to one side will affect the other two; as a result, they are often managed together.

Plan Scope, Time, and Cost

Scope answers the question "How much work must I get done?" This constraint is a funny one. It's where many people get tripped up. Go back to the elephant I mentioned earlier, and think about each bite it takes to eat it. Those bites identify all the work that has to be done by defining the output of that work (deliverables) to accomplish the project goal.

The scope of a project can be difficult to nail down because there are so many ways to describe the final outcome. Unless the goal is clear, the steps to get there will be a challenge to define. Similar to how uncertainty in vision leads to an unclear strategy, ambiguous objectives lead to missed goals. For example, your objective may be "I'd like to a write a book," but this statement is ambiguous because the type of book matters—memoir, resource, cookbook, and so on. Defining a big bucket is an easy way to score in a basketball game, but it's not helpful in setting goals.

Often this vagueness occurs because you're trying to anticipate changes, but there is a better way to handle that anticipation. IT introduced a software development method called Agile that defines the bites we're going to take based on the time we have allotted. Each predefined interval is intended to have a working release of software whose final scope is not fully determined. We eventually get to the elephant (or final result) by iterating through all the work. Its foundation is in the process of *inspect and adapt* after each interval, giving it structure and flexibility. The Agile approach came about because of the rapid nature of changes and uncertainty in business and to accommodate our instant-gratification tendencies. You can account for shifting priorities, and you get to see incremental progress. Often the result is having something useable much faster, which allows you to respond to customer needs. Have you ever wondered why your iPhone keeps prompting you to update your apps? The app developers in the iTunes store use Agile.

Whether you define your scope using a traditional goal-setting method or you account for more uncertainty and use an Agile approach, you will still need to have a defined outcome and a task list that accompanies it.

Time (schedule) answers two questions: "How long will this take?" and, if given a deadline, "Can I accomplish my goal in the time frame that is specified?" You arrive at your completion date by adding up the time it will take to complete all the steps to accomplish your goal. If you have decided to acquire a new certification, you will have to add up the time it takes for the required training, study time, and other obligations that may arise. This will give you a schedule to follow.

You can also arrive at a schedule by taking a finish date and working backward. Practically speaking, this is how most event-based projects are planned. You are given an event date, and the actions needed to pull it together are all weighed against the amount of time you have to complete them. Ever arrive at a wedding wondering what all the fuss in the back is about? Chances are someone had too much to do and too little time.

In life change, this equates to understanding how much additional time you have to devote to a new skill or to determining if there is a pressing date. As I prepared for my trip to Africa, I reviewed my Spanish, knowing that I had a limited time to study (the trip was organized in less than six weeks) and that I had professional and personal obligations that were taking a considerable amount of my time. Thank goodness for Rosetta Stone!

Likewise, if you have decided that you want to train for a race, you would reverse engineer your schedule to account for race day and create a training schedule with that in mind. If, however, the goal you have set for yourself is to lose weight (or inches), you would evaluate a realistic and healthy rate of weight loss and determine how long it will take you to reach your goal based on that rate. I wouldn't recommend arbitrarily stating, "I will lose *x* number of pounds (or inches) in *y* amount of time," as that leads to unrealistic expectations and frustration.

Cost (budget) answers the question "How much money will this cost?" This constraint forces you to look at your financial situation and consider how you will fund the endeavor. Can you accomplish your goals given the funds that you have available? Will your employer pay for your degree, or will you have to pay out of pocket?

The cost of a project is the sum of the cost of labor (or human resources) assigned to the work plus any additional materials or equipment. If you are pursuing a certification, advanced degree, or other educational growth opportunity, you have to factor in the cost of tuition, books, and transportation. These can easily add up, so you need to include a way of measuring them during the project.

One of my favorite New Testament reminders, found in Luke 14:28, is to "count the cost." The cost of a personal or professional change initiative isn't always money; it also includes other life-altering changes such as your energy and emotions. When you look at time and cost together, you can make determinations as to how much money, time, and energy you'll need to budget. This dimension often drives the decision of whether those pursuing advanced degrees do so in the evenings or if they take a break from work to go back to school full time. Add up all the components to develop your budget.

Keep in mind that your budget and schedule can be impacted by risk. Risks are uncertain events that could impact your project. In order to have an accurate plan that you can follow, you need to account for risks by listing what they may be and analyzing the impact they will have on your project if they were to occur. You'll want to have a contingency plan (a plan B) in place for your high-priority risks, while the others you can just take in stride. Only you can determine your risk tolerance when it comes to meeting your goals. Ask yourself, "What will happen to my goal if this happens?"

As the name implies, the Triple Constraint has three sides, but there are far more than three forces at work in a project. That's when I walk up to the board and put a big *Q* smack dab in the middle of the triangle. The *Q* stands for quality, and it's in the middle because it doesn't get adjusted or negotiated like the three sides. Quality is nonnegotiable. If you're going to do it, do it well!

The discipline of shaping these three sides while maintaining quality is the foundation of project management. There is far more to it, and I get an absolute kick out of teaching it in detail to aspiring and veteran project managers. I've got interesting articles on my website providing insight into various key areas of project management and navigating change. The aim at this point is to simplify project planning so that you can apply it to your everyday life.

To review, to keep the project triangle in balance, define a scope of work that can be accomplished with the time you have and with the money you are willing to spend. It always starts with scope because that is the foundation for your project. Look back to one of the goals you established in Step 1, Decide. Now break that up into actionable steps to create a task list—your work breakdown structure (WBS). For instance, if you decided you wanted to pursue a PMP certification, you would define the steps required by the governing organization (the Project Management Institute, or PMI) and how long each step would take. You would have to:

- review application requirements

- schedule training

- attend training

- complete an application

- remit the funds

- receive application approval

- schedule the exam

- prepare for the exam

- take (and pass) the exam

As you would find out by walking through this process, there are tasks that are dependent on others. For example, you can't schedule the exam until your application has been approved, and you can't take the exam until you schedule it. Once you identify the logical order of the work you need to do, you can add up the durations based on the sequence you came up with, and you have your schedule. To accurately determine how long an individual activity will take (the duration), you also have to factor in uncertainty (risks) and your other work and personal commitments (your allocation).

Last, add up the cost of training, the application fee, and any other resources you use to study for the exam. Summarize these costs, and you have your budget. The online guide includes sample WBSs (task lists) for this goal and several other useful goals, including writing a book, training for a 5K, or developing more emotional intelligence.

CHAPTER 9

Do the Work

...

Comedian Larry the Cable Guy popularized the expression "Get 'er done" in his popular 1990s stand-up routine. The phrase prompts you to get moving. It has made its way into common vernacular when someone wants something done now and doesn't want you to make a "project" out of it. This is a harmless sentiment when you're fixing a flat tire or running a report. However, being in a rush to get something done without making a plan first can be to your detriment when embarking on implementing your goals at work or at home. You get to this third step, Do, only after you devise a plan; don't start here, or you could set yourself up for disaster.

Work the Plan

Now that you have a well-thought-out plan that accounts for uncertainty (risks) and identifies how you will handle deviations from the plan, you can get to work. When you follow your car's navigation system, it prevents you from making wrong turns by telling you the best route. If you do make a wrong turn, it reroutes you back on your path and informs you of your new arrival time. While you are actively doing, you refer to your plan like you follow your GPS, using it to get you back on track.

Like your trusty GPS, you have to collect data along the way that you can use to monitor your progress. Depending on your goal and your schedule, you may need to analyze this information daily. As you keep a watchful eye out for differences between what you are actually doing and what you had planned to do (your variances), you can manage your expectations and those of anyone depending on the completion of this goal.

Set Up Milestones and Rewards

One great technique to keep you on track is to use milestones. These are often used to report progress and reasons to celebrate. The term originated in ancient Rome where they placed large boulders at each mile throughout the Roman Empire. Soldiers then knew how far they were from the city (or a battleground). In modern times, we see mile markers on freeways that serve the same purpose. In your project plans, milestones help pave the way to success by showing you the completion of major objectives within your larger project. They also let you know if you've kept in step with your plan and can help signify delays and needs to adjust. Set up your personal accountability and rewards to align with your milestones.

Learn to Adapt

Your plan will change, your life will change, and your motivations may change. But if you measure your progress along the way, you will be much more likely to accomplish your goals.

If circumstances change in the middle of Step 3, Do, then go back to your plan and make adjustments based on the new information. I caution you here to not abandon your plan but rather adapt it to your evolving situation. If you found yourself missing your original deadline, set a new one. Once you've agreed with yourself on your new deadline, reschedule all the remaining work to get there.

Since your plan includes more than the schedule, pay close attention to your Triple Constraint t to ensure that it doesn't get out of balance and that quality doesn't suffer. If you have to hurry to accomplish your goal in less time, you may need to increase your budget to account for it; you can't have it both ways.

Looking again at the example of working toward a certification, the Do step in the Four-Step Strategic Change Leadership model involves following the road map that you laid out in the previous Devise step. You would need to study according to the schedule that you set forth, committing yourself to that work so that you can take the examination on or around the date you specified. As you monitor your progress, you can ensure that you'll be prepared by your test date; otherwise, you can reschedule it to account for delays in your preparation. I particularly like this example because it is often a self-imposed deadline, and those who don't follow their own schedule often regret not heeding that advice. Examinations change and knowledge atrophies, so making and sticking to a plan is one way to ensure you will meet the goal. If your goal is to become a certified PMP, it is another opportunity to practice what you preach: Decide, Devise, Do, and Review!

CHAPTER 10

Review the Outcome

• • •

The fourth and final step of the Four-Step Strategic Change Leadership model is Review. When you near the completion of your goal, you should begin reflecting on how closely you achieved your objective. Because transformation is a series of changes, you may need to review your results to determine what, if anything, you need to do to continue to improve. If you've set a specific goal—for instance, a certification—you can review your test results to determine if your plan and following that plan yielded the results you needed. If you passed the test, then there is nothing more to do there. If you fell short of a passing score, however, you will need to review what you missed and retake the exam.

Remember What Success Looks Like

Every race has a clearly defined finish line. Likewise, your personal goals have a definition of success to measure against during execution and upon completion. In the Decide step, you had to define what success looks like. So, when you review the outcome, measure it against your predetermined success criteria to know if you can declare victory.

The same holds true for major projects. The health of a project is determined by certain measured parameters, called key performance indicators (KPIs). These key points are useful in helping an organization determine its successes and failures. A KPI is a quantifiable measure that gauges performance in terms of meeting certain strategic and operational goals, whether those goals relate to personal achievements or corporate ones. KPIs must be aligned with your objectives.

If your decision was to run a 5K race (3.1 miles), you will have created and followed a training plan to get you to race day. When you cross the finish line, you can immediately see your race time. Once you've had a banana and lots of water, you can ask yourself, "Is this the result I wanted?" If you answer no, then evaluate what you could have done differently to give you a different outcome. Were there unexpected hills? Was the wind at your face? Did you trail off in your training plan toward the end? Any of these could have contributed to not achieving your desired result. If the answer is yes, then review the steps you took to get there and enjoy the celebration.

In both cases (goal attained or goal missed), find someone to share your lessons learned with. As Rick Warren points out in *The Purpose Driven Life*, "It's not about you."

I'm a movie fan, but I'm married to a movie buff. Trust me, there is a big difference! One movie we both thoroughly enjoyed is *National Lampoon's Vacation*. The movie is hilarious (and at times completely inappropriate), but it makes a really good point. In the movie, the family patriarch, Clark Griswold (played by Chevy Chase), is determined to plan a great vacation for his family so they can bond on the trip and grow closer. He has a great vision, and he creates a plan with great detail. Bless his heart, though; his plan is flawed and is foiled at many points throughout the movie. The lesson in this movie is that when your car explodes or runs off the road, grab your things and your family and get back on your path. He demonstrates true resilience in his ability to bounce back from each setback in the trip (and there are many). At the end, when they arrive at Walley World only to find it is closed for repairs, the audience is reminded how important fact gathering is for any project! Creating a plan without all the facts can create unintended results. Remember the technicians in Malabo? You have to put your head down, solve the problem, and capture your lessons learned for next time.

The great thing about devising an iterative plan is that you continue to improve with each iteration, gradually getting to the measure of success you defined. Some goals are "one and done," meaning you start them, you accomplish them, and you celebrate. Others are a series of successes (and failures) that get you to your desired result over time. You may have made the distinction in the Devise phase, but your results will ultimately determine if you need a redo or if you need to make plans for the next goal.

Did You Succeed?

Now let's apply this to the strategic plan you created. You started with a decision, and that decision was tied to your vision and your purpose. From there you defined a long-term strategy. This is something in the distance that you can see clearly—something you can accomplish if you put your mind and your heart to it. You may have put it on a vision board so you can see it, so you can commit to it and hold yourself accountable. Next, you devised your plan based on that vision, thinking through the steps you need. Part of the planning process is elaborating on "What is success?" and measuring against that definition at regular intervals. While you are in the Do phase, you need to refer to the KPIs you established so you can ensure you are on track. Once you reach Review, you can ensure that your goal was attained, or you can go back to Decide to take it to the next level, gradually reaching your desired state. The completion of one goal is an opportunity to start new ones. That is how strategic life change takes place.

PART 3

Keep Your Focus

• • •

What you focus on grows.

—Robin S. Sharma

The imperatives you defined in Part 2 are part of a long-term vision. To keep focus on that vision, you'll need to give them priority and watch them closely.

Keeping focus becomes an issue when first implementing change and continues to wreak havoc while trying to sustain the change.

The following strategies will help you maintain focus:

- Get Some Bifocals

- Be Intentional

- Put Up Guardrails

- Build Your Resilience

- Watch Your Balance

CHAPTER 11

Get Some Bifocals

• • •

One of the most difficult challenges in our busy world is maintaining focus on our long-term goals. When I turned forty, my optometrist explained to me that my eyes were weakening and that I should get some bifocals. I agreed, but only if he called them "progressives"!

He went on to explain that progressives allow me to see straight ahead to a far distance with clarity, but if I need to read something close (like my phone), I can just lower my eyes, and the prescription changes. This means I can manage two views while looking in the same direction. Then he warned me that if I looked out of the corner of my eyes (taking my eyes off what is in front of me), my vision will be blurry. When I'm driving, my progressives allow me to see ahead to the destination, and they allow me to quickly adjust my sight to read the details on my phone that will help me arrive safely. This happens while allowing me to know other cars are around me and limiting distractions. As a trained tractor-trailer driver, I know the importance of moving my head to check my mirrors and to be aware of my surroundings, but I don't let objects in my mirror deter my progress.

This dual prescription allows me to see the vision and long-term goals that have been set in front of me and the details I need to accomplish them, but it hinders the sight of distractions from the side.

The same holds true for the focus you must maintain when sustaining growth and change in your life. You have to keep your eyes fixed on a long-term vision to clearly see what the destination or endgame will look like. You also have to be able to focus on the details of the work that needs to be done while minimizing distractions.

Once I recognized my catalyst and crafted a vision statement to go along with it, I knew I had a lot of work to do to accomplish my goals. When I created my personal growth plan to include personal spiritual growth, work and home leadership, and professional development, I was only at the beginning. Using the model, I converted my vision into a series of action plans, but it was my commitment to the plans that made the difference.

This dual focus became the driving force behind my home-based consultancy. Being able to envision myself as the business leader I aspired to be kept me focused on the future. A slight shift of my eyes allowed me to see the professional development steps I would need to take to get there. There was so much to learn, and I was excited about it. Business formation, tax structure, hiring, client relations, and marketing were all areas that I needed to firmly establish for a successful business.

Each year I had to prioritize my business and professional development goals—while maintaining the progress I had made in my spiritual and personal growth. Additionally, the peripheral blurring helped minimize distractions when other less relevant opportunities presented themselves. For example, my future focus encouraged me to pursue DISC certification as a necessary step toward understand human behavior for myself and my clients.

Bifocal vision allows you to keep your eyes on the prize while working diligently to get there.

CHAPTER 12

Be Intentional

• • •

I love the adage "What you focus on grows." It speaks to intentionally investing your time and attention in the things that matter. And in return, you'll earn dividends. Most often, people focus on the important relationships, tasks, and projects in their lives, but that can be difficult. There are so many things vying for your attention and competing for your energy and focus. This can be especially frustrating when we talk about goals. Making goals is important, but sticking to them is even more vital.

Here are a few strategies you can employ as you work to maintain your focus.

Put First Things First

As Dr. Covey states in *The 7 Habits of Highly Effective People*, "The main thing is to keep the main thing the main thing." Put the important things in your life (or day) at the top of your to-do list. Focus on completing those things before you dive into something else.

I found this principle especially helpful in prioritizing my strategic imperatives. I'm a lover of learning, so there are so many things I want to learn and do, but this principle reminded me to create plans that focus on growing in the most important areas and completing tasks associated with that growth first. It is also a helpful principle for maintaining work-life balance and encourages us to begin with what matters most to us.

If I find myself trying to do too many things at once, I pause and ask myself, "Is this the most important thing today?" Then I redirect myself if the answer warrants it. Ultimately, coaching myself to use Stephen Covey's principles of effectiveness have kept me focused and able to accomplish more.

Drown Out the Noise

Distractions are all around us. Even the best-laid-out day can be filled with calls, emails, and other matters that take your focus away. Try methods like the Pomodoro Technique (which has an app for your phone) to manage your productive times. The app coaches you to focus intentionally during an interval of productivity and then take a break. This did wonders for me and kept me from chasing squirrels in my mind (when my I style takes over) and from becoming too immersed (when my C style takes hold).

When I have focus-intensive work to do, I turn off my ringer, and I check my email at predetermined intervals. Being intentional about drowning out distractions for a set amount of time allows me to focus on the vision and the action steps to get there. You'll find that you get to cross more things off your to-do list (if you're in the Do phase) and that your plans are more comprehensive (if you're in the Devise phase) when you set aside undistracted time.

The reason most people have difficulty with distraction is because they have bought into the myth of multitasking. Yes, the human brain is capable of handling multiple thoughts at once, but only one will receive your true focus. For instance, I love to listen to music when I run. I realize that I can either focus on the music or focus on my pace. Sometimes the music is just in the background as I coach myself, and sometimes I'm cruising on autopilot while I pay close attention to the lyrics.

Create a Time-Sensitive, Visual Plan

I like vision boards, but they only remind us of what our visions are and neglect when we want to accomplish each task. While you may be saying, "Here goes Ms. Project Manager again," I must say that creating a visual time line of tasks and goals alongside your visions will help you stay focused. There are tons of tools that will let you create something electronically, and having that in a smartphone app will allow you to access your plan wherever you are so you can be constantly reminded. The key is to open the app!

Because opening an app sometimes eludes us in our busyness, I'm still a proponent of keeping it old school. Sometimes it's even better is to print out your time line, put it somewhere visible, and mentally check in with it. Printing a Gantt chart or a time line image is an excellent way to keep your subconscious brain focused on your conscious tasks.

Set Up an Accountability System

The visual plan you created is useful for keeping you accountable, but sharing its contents (your milestones, etc.) with someone else is the key to accountability. Whether it's your spouse, a friend, a prayer partner, or a mastermind group, sharing your goals (the *what* and the *when*) will help you remain focused on the promise you made to yourself. As you set up your goals, be sure to add an accountability partner to keep you focused on achieving them.

I am a fan of mastermind groups, and I attribute the release of my memoir to being part of one. I had a visual plan with my tasks and milestones, but having the added accountability to follow my plan was priceless. I find the same benefit in group health classes. I'm not nearly as social while I'm running or doing Zumba, but keeping up with others is encouraging, and the conversations post workout can be downright inspiring.

The online companion guide has great tips and resources to help you maintain your focus while working through your goals. Whether it's your health, your wealth, or your relationships, you'll need to focus to make them grow because if you don't, they won't.

CHAPTER 13

Put Up Guardrails

• • •

I enjoy the life teachings of Andy Stanley, a pastor from Atlanta, Georgia. He has a video series titled *Guardrails* in which he shares the importance of guardrails in our lives. He begins by reminding us of the practical use of the guardrails that we see on the side of the road—the ones that are designed to keep us from falling into the ditch. He clarifies that in life, the standards, rules, and principles that you follow serve as your guardrails.

In the broader picture of who we are (or our vision for who we want to become), our guardrails hold us to a threshold of habits and choices that maintain our integrity. When you make a decision about you are, guardrails help you adhere to it. They may come in the form of questions that you pose to yourself or clearly written dos and don'ts. For example, as a married woman, I have a guardrail that I won't dine with a man that my husband doesn't know well. In the case of business meetings with a man, I use caution and ensure that the conversation has a clear purpose and sticks to it.

As we pursue our life-change initiatives, it's important for us to put up guardrails that help us decide how we'll achieve and maintain our goals. If you're in school and you're studying, one guardrail might be to not attend more than one social event during the week and instead use that time to complete your coursework.

That would have been a great guardrail for me when I was in college, but I digress. If you've grown in your spiritual practice, one guardrail might be to read a devotional (or your Bible) daily. Your convictions can help you stay on track, even if your friends or family are enticing you to do otherwise.

Ultimately, these thresholds help us maintain a commitment we've made to ourselves or to others. Because your goals are personal to your purpose, passion, and priorities, they may not look the same as other people's goals. For that reason, one guardrail to put in place is to avoid comparing your success to the success of others. They may have different goals and capacities in their lives. At one point, I began to get antsy about growing my business because I compared myself to other business owners, but my business had a specific mission, which was to allow me to work from home. Through Andy Stanley's video series, I became acquainted with a verse from Nehemiah 6:3: "I'm doing a great work and I can't come down. Why should the work come to a standstill just so I can come down to see you?" It reinforced my commitment to being a work-from-home mom when my children were young, and guides my business goals even as they get older

This also takes you back to the "Is this the season?" question you asked and answered. Your guardrails will be a function of your season of life and your circumstances. It is important to be true to who you are. If you have determined that you need to care for your aging parents, then the professional commitments you make may need to be adjusted to account for that need.

If a goal you have established for yourself involves your health, your physician has likely given you some guardrails. These boundaries were established to keep your health measurements in optimal condition. Once I reached my goal weight and body mass index a year after giving birth to my youngest son, I knew there were certain foods I needed to avoid. Maintaining that weight loss for years to come was a priority for me, so the guardrails weren't considered a hindrance—they were a help.

When we remember that the guardrails on the highways are there to help us, establishing them in our lives is easy. Guardrails help you stay in your lane—whatever that lane may be. Ask yourself, "What kind of guardrails do I need to put in place?"

CHAPTER 14

Build Your Resilience

. . .

During the course of our lives, all of us are forced into change. Character, however, is determined not by the challenges we endure but how we recover from them. I often advise others to journal as they reflect, release, and realize defining moments in their lives. In my first two books, *Love Is a Catalyst* and *Love Is a Catalyst: The Pain behind the Purpose*, I chronicle significant moments in my life, such as my mother's untimely death, my oldest son's battle with cancer, and my struggle as a young engineer in the oil field. These and other moments helped me learn to overcome adversity and build my personal resilience.

Resilience is a muscle that we have many opportunities to strengthen, and storms have a way of teaching us how to be resilient. The storms in life (both literal and figurative) bring destruction, and our ability to bounce back is developed each time we recover.

Weather Storms Like Knock Out Roses

At the advice of my landscaper, I planted Knock Out roses in my front yard and backyard when I moved into my new home in 2014. I researched them before planting them, and I knew they were a hybrid, genetically engineered for harsh conditions. They were touted for their resilience, and I loved having rose blooms year-round with the occasional dormancy. I could sit on my back porch or in the breakfast nook and stare at them for hours. Their beauty was unmatched, and I appreciated their hardiness.

When Hurricane Harvey hit the Texas Gulf Coast in 2017, their natural resilience was put to the test. My husband, my youngest son, and I were at home riding out the storm. We watched anxiously as water filled the street and began its way up the driveway. We kept watch all night, taking turns watching the water pass markers we had placed in the driveway. As the heavy rainfall continued, the polluted floodwater from the street began to spill into our yard and threatened our home. Thankfully, the elevation of our house kept the rising water from getting to the door and subsequently inside, but watching it all night gave us quite a scare. The next morning, we were relieved to see the water beginning to slowly recede. Standing on my front porch, I could smell the stench of the stagnant water, and I could see the debris it was leaving behind. I thought for sure my Knock Out rosebushes were goners.

I consulted my new lawn service provider (my original landscaper died of cancer shortly after planting my landscape), and he urged me to just cut them back as we normally did and wait to see what would happen. They looked weak and sad and had been through quite an ordeal, but I took his advice. I waited patiently for the spring, and to my amazement, the Knock Out roses in the front and back came back just as strong as they had in previous years. These roses did exactly what they were engineered to do—they recovered! As photos I took proved, they fulfilled their purpose by filling my yard with radiant shades of red and pink.

When the roses recovered from the flood after Hurricane Harvey, they proved they could thrive through harsh conditions. They had already proven themselves to be drought resistant and able to withstand the intense sun; now they added polluted water to their resume. The quick freezes that we experience continue to give them a pop quiz, but through it all, they bounce back time after time. We have to do that in life. It's not enough to come back from one difficult situation; resilience is about withstanding adversity time and again.

I can't tell you how many times I've had to recover my business, restore a relationship, or renew a commitment. Each time I do, my muscles get stronger, and my resilience gets further developed. On my journey to spiritual transformation, I have been set back by the loss of numerous loved ones, my son, Malcolm in 2014, being the most difficult to endure. The same year that I lost Malcolm to cancer, the bottom fell out of the oil and gas industry, and new clients were extremely hard to find. Add to it that my husband also worked in the same industry—the intestinal fortitude it took to rebuild my business in the midst of that kind of uncertainty was unmatched.

But I had a vision to focus on and the hope to keep me going. As I've learned, resilience is rooted in optimism. It's based on the hope that your efforts will get you back on track. Resilience requires the ability to focus on what you are trying to rebuild while it is still destroyed. In my life, that has been my home, my family, my physical and emotional health, and my business.

I want to give special thanks to Gary L. Selman, who helped me recover from that tragic season. I sought professional help in the aftermath of losing my son, but I found that regaining momentum was more difficult than I'd hoped. Gary helped me connect the dots between my faith and my professional goals. His coaching and the introduction to workplace ministry helped me recover from ashes.

Explore Your Closet

Your closet of life lessons is likely full of stories and situations where you had to recover from difficult situations. And as you explored your closet earlier in this book, you were likely discouraged by the disappointment it contains. Hopefully, however, you are encouraged by the strength you gained from those experiences. As you replay your life story, each of those experiences added to your resilience and provided insight into how you respond in certain situations. As you explored your wounds, you may have discovered that you are more resilient than you realize. If your searching your heart uncovered that you recover slowly and struggle to get back on track after challenges, plug that variable back into the Decide, Devise, Do, and Review steps and create a growth plan.

CHAPTER 15

Watch Your Balance

• • •

Work-life balance is an issue for every working adult. It is often implied that maintaining a work-life balance is only necessary for people with children. In reality, we all need balance and activities that feed our spirits, minds, bodies, and hearts. As you work and focus on your goals, it's important to not lose balance in your life. When you factor costs into your planning, take into consideration the affect that your high-priority career goal will have on your personal life and vice versa. You can have it all, but not always at the same time.

Stop Doing Too Much

Keep this principle in mind when deciding how many goals you will commit to. Having too many goals is equivalent to not having any goals. If you find yourself unable to keep pace with the goals you set, review and prioritize them. You many need to defer some for another time, or you may find that the ones you're giving priority to aren't really your top priorities. Be adaptable in your plans, and be on the lookout for signs of burnout that indicate you're taking on too much.

Get Rid of Worry and Fear, the Energy-Draining Twins

In a typical week, most people spend 50 percent of their waking hours at work, 23 percent with family, 10 percent on personal goals, 8 percent on leisure, and 9 percent on fear and doubt. These numbers are not scientific, but they do illustrate the amount of wasted energy we put into worrying about outcomes, doubting our abilities, and fearing the future. If this negative energy were eliminated (or at least minimized), you would have more room to focus on what really matters.

Your catalyst has the power to keep you focused on what you will accomplish even when doubt sets in. It keeps you encouraged when fear tries to stop you, and it keeps you hopeful when you want to worry. When you live a life driven by passion and purpose, you focus on significance over success.

After I left Schlumberger, I took a position as a program manager at a small IT company. Thankfully this firm used Salesforce, so I had the opportunity to attend Dreamforce, which is a conference where Salesforce users are inspired to change the world (and use technology). After hearing retired four-star general Colin Powell speak on servant leadership and Salesforce CEO Marc Benoit highlight the benefits of corporate philanthropy, I heard my calling.

I gave my notice and returned to the consultancy that I had created a few months prior but was too afraid to operate. In 2006, after a life-changing encounter with God in my "closet," I moved forward. As a result, I was able to spend more time with my family while working at home. I took the leap of faith into entrepreneurship and found it to be uplifting. The balance it gives me emotionally and spiritually is priceless.

At the end of the day, what matters most to me is my family, including my husband, Rodney, and our sons. For me, raising four boys to be men of purpose took love, strength, and lots of time. I couldn't let fear keep me from doing what was best for them and for me.

When it comes to our life plans, we are stepping into the unknown. We have to be willing to take risks, evaluate outcomes, and make quick adjustments. The most astute planners realize that they can't account for every possible scenario, so the process has to include a few "what if" scenarios. For me, I had to ask myself the following questions: What if my business doesn't make any money? What if I fail? What if I succeed? While there are safeguards you can put in place to prevent negative outcomes, there is no guarantee, and that's where faith comes in.

Regardless of your spiritual practice, the notion of being able to excel even in the face of uncertainty is powerful. There will always be things in life that we can't control, and true peace comes when we accept that truth. Successful people have faith. Regardless of spiritual practice, faith is a belief that your future will be better than your present. Otherwise what are you working toward? Believe. Succeed. Have faith.

A few years after starting my consultancy, I had finally created the balance I so desired. My clients were receiving the quality service I prided myself on delivering. I had a great team, and I had set hours. That last part is important because, during start-up, I seemed to work around the clock responding to email and building my business. But the emphasis on my priorities gave me a reason to get that right. My boys were in three different schools, and I was actively involved in each school (two boys were in high school, one was in middle school, and one was in elementary school). I felt like I needed superpowers. I recharged my powers on weekends with dancing or going to a movie with my husband. Mine was a delicately balanced life.

I remember reading a quote: "How you do one thing is how you do everything, beware" (author unknown). This quote epitomized balance for me. I proudly added it to my email signature. Unfortunately, I allowed pride to get in the way and, thinking I could handle the extra load, took on more work. Eventually, the scales of balance tipped, and I found myself running late to everything.

On one occasion, I attempted to cancel a commitment for a board that I served on. Rob, the president of the board, responded by quoting my signature line. His comment was in jest, but he was right! Like my uncle's "Or is there?" Rob's email challenged me to regain my balance.

Life Is Not a Juggle; It's a Balance

Notice I said "balance" and not "juggle." I've never been a fan of the phrase "life is a juggle" because in most cases we can't put something down—everything has to remain on the scale. For instance, no matter how important a project at work was, I was always a mom first. Most days that balance worked out, but if a child was sick or had an important life event, the scale tipped. If a project had a major milestone approaching, the scale would tip in that direction. Life teeter-totters daily.

What things are you balancing? Marriage? Children? Aging parents? Pets? Personal activities? Ask yourself, "What things are important to me, and how do I keep them in balance?"

PART 4

Sharpen Someone Else

• • •

As iron sharpens iron, so one man sharpens another.

—Proverbs 27:17

Using your catalyst to keep you focused on maintaining your progress and to sustain what you have already accomplished is only part of its power. Use it to fuel your servant leadership. Your success and achievements are not about you; they are about the people in your life that you can impact as a result of them. That's living in your purpose.

You can change the world by:

- Leading Change in Your Family

- Leading Change in Your Community

- Leading Change in Your Organization

CHAPTER 16
Lead Change in Your Family

• • •

There's no place like home to put into practice the principals and strategies for effective change leadership. Families look very different and come in all shapes and sizes, but they all need leadership, and they all need a vision.

Early in our marriage, Rodney and I created a family vision: our family will impact the kingdom by raising future husbands to be men of faith, service, and respect. That then translated into our mission statement: we're raising future husbands. As we planned our annual family calendar, we took our family vision and mission into account and ensured the boys were academically enriched, served in their church and community, and were respectful at school and at home—I loved watching people's faces when all four would respond "Yes, ma'am" to a request.

It was this mission statement that challenged me when I arrived home from my West Africa trip. Our family had been challenged with the epitome of blended-family issues: estrangement. It was heartbreaking, and leading up to my trip, I hadn't been able to see or talk to my older boys in four months. I had decided from day one to be an involved stepmom and to love my boys as if they were my own, so this estrangement cut me to my core. Our family had been torn apart because of bitterness, anger, and deceit. It was going to take a miracle to rebuild it, but I was ready!

While I was on the Paris leg of the West Africa trip, we had a breakthrough. I was standing in front of the Sacré-Coeur when my husband called to tell me contact had been made! I cried tears of joy, and then I compartmentalized my feelings to complete my audit trip. When I returned home, we were ready to make moves. Dusting off the feelings of helplessness that had paralyzed us, my husband and I prayed and put a plan in place to restore our family. As much as the separation hurt, it was our catalyst to put in the work to restore our family not to what it was before but an even better version!

Conducting a "Know Your Family" assessment will help uncover strengths, weaknesses, and areas for growth in your family just as it did for your personal life. You will find a template on www.WhatsYourCatalyst.com. Use the DISC model to identify the behavioral and communication styles of your family, and chart them together. This is a great exercise that will allow you to see where you complement one another and where you might clash. Remember, this a tool, not a weapon! Use the results to help you communicate with your family members more effectively and not belittle their differences. Does conflict escalate into battles? Does planning the family vacation require everyone to cater to any one person's needs?

Once you define what those growth areas are, you can move ahead to create and sustain the change you need. Just as in your own growth plan, it starts with a vision. Spend time in prayer or meditation reflecting on the vision you want for your family. Iterate through it with your spouse and see what you come up with. Involve your children so they will also have ownership. Ask yourself, "What is our family purposed to do? What's keeping us from doing it?"

Next, apply **the Four-Step Strategic Change Leadership model** to the key goals you establish for your family's growth.

Apply the same advice and warnings about measurements, thresholds, and balance that you used in your personal growth plan. Your family will need accomplishments celebrated and progress acknowledged. They will also need to take corrective action when deviations occur.

The average American family only eats dinner together three to four times a week, and the effect that has on closeness and communication is clear. The American Academy of Pediatrics has published several studies on the effects of family dinners on children. Simply taking charge of having meals together will allow your family members the opportunity to discuss their days and share in family life. Even families with the best of intentions can fall into this pattern. The good news is with so many options available, being able to cook is no longer a prerequisite! Decide that your family will break bread together.

It could be that your family doesn't manage conflict very well. You're not alone. The stress placed on families today has significantly contributed to heightened, unhealthy conflict. I specify "unhealthy" conflict because conflict itself is neither good nor bad. Conflict means having different perspectives and ideas, and what teenagers don't have different perspectives from their parents? The problem arises when conflict escalates and becomes fighting, arguing, and yelling.

I have a confession: I am a recovering yeller. While it may sound morbid, I have found that one way to catch myself in my anger is to remind myself of how I handled issues when my eldest son was battling cancer. I was careful, I spoke gently, and I relayed the truth in love. There was so much at stake (a dangerously ill son, worried brothers, and an anxious husband). Compassion flowed freely, and I extended grace by the truckload. I was so filled with the love my faith granted me that even though I was stressed, I was steady. My auntie taught me about "hushed-mouth grace," and I had to learn to put that lesson into practice even when there wasn't a diagnosis looming over anyone. Listening empathically is not something that comes naturally to me, so I have to work on it. Some days the work yields the results I want; other days are, well, a work in progress.

Your family may not be challenged with a life-threatening illness, but the hearts and minds of your children are incredibly fragile. Providing them with love and limits will help develop them into responsible, caring adults and will keep you from overreacting.

If you find yourself needing to heal your family from unhealthy conflict, discord, or dysfunction, applying the Four-Step Strategic Change Leadership model will give you a framework to build on. Once you make the decision, devise a plan, which may require resources outside your home. Books and training programs are great, and you may also need the help of a licensed professional to guide your family. Involve your children in the planning and get their buy-in. This will teach them how to use the model in their own lives. Reaffirm your vision for a healthy family, and create a plan to get there.

Once you've created a plan, confirm that everyone in your family understands it. Was one of your goals to eat at home more often? Consider setting a schedule, and include who gets to pick the meal each night. If you find your family needs to reduce strife and have more productive disagreements, your plan may include resources to learn conflict resolution. During the Do step, be sure to reward those who collaborate well. Use the online Family Collaboration Chart at www.WhatsYourCatalyst.com.

Whether you are in a single-parent household, a two-parent household, or a blended family, being able to value the contributions of your family members is incredibly important. Lead the charge in that effort.

CHAPTER 17

Lead Change in Your Community

• • •

One of the most rewarding places that your change leadership skills can be utilized is in your own community. This can come in the form of volunteering your professional skills and your talents to benefit those around you. Depending on your leadership style, you may feel compelled to spearhead efforts for continuous improvement.

When my boys where school age, I volunteered with the parent-teacher association at their schools. I soon found it helpful to assume leadership roles where I could utilize my leadership, communication, and project-management skills. Especially important was the ability to evaluate success on one campus and to mirror that on other campuses.

One year, I noticed a dilemma at my youngest son's school. He was in the third grade and was becoming more active and socially independent. He was a passionate reader, and he liked being dropped off at school early so he could sit and read. I think he also liked being the "line leader," a designation given to the early arrivers. The school had a small gym and one physical education (PE) teacher, so as a result, my rambunctious eight-year-old only had PE once every five days! He and the other balls of energy were becoming a lot to handle in the classrooms, and his teachers weren't always able to provide solutions. Add to that the fact that the childhood obesity data for the school had come in, and there was a problem. The after-lunch recess they had just wasn't enough.

I noticed a need, and after conducting some research, I approached the principal with a proposal to start a before-school fitness/wellness program. The program's goal was simply to get the kids to move for twenty minutes and then settle them down with a nutrition lesson. Given that it was volunteer led, we limited it to two days a week. They learned about healthy portions and basic anatomy after a fun Zumba session. I branded the program "Blue Jays in Motion" with a tagline that a blue jay in motion tends to stay in motion (see how I added some science there).

The application of the Decide, Devise, Do, and Review steps to this initiative was most relevant for the last step—Review. I worked with the district's wellness coordinator to review the program's effectiveness. Our goal was to provide a blueprint for other schools to implement similar programs and, of course, to continue it at my son's elementary school for subsequent third graders. The anecdotal evidence about the children's behavior and focus on days with the program was indisputable. Even on days without the program, teachers could leverage the children's love for the program and threaten to deduct time for misbehavior.

The program got the attention of the community at large, and the students, our volunteer Zumba instructor, and I performed in the plaza at a local wellness festival. The school received grants and awards for the program, and the children gained valuable encouragement. Other schools began to take note of ways to incorporate fitness activity into other functions, and we saw a spike in fun runs and field-day participants across the district. Unfortunately, the program lacked the volunteer availability to sustain it after that year, but its impact was highly celebrated.

Serving in this capacity reminded me of the joy I felt when I started the clothing drive for the children in Africa. Efforts great and small have an impact on the people around us. Ask yourself, "How can I use my talents to lead change in my community?"

You don't have to be "in charge" to make an impact on your community. Leadership is not about a position; it is combination of character traits that bring out the best in others. Depending on your DISC style, you may be more comfortable "leading from behind," meaning you may prefer to be a strong team player, enacting the vision of the leader by being an outstanding participant in the initiative. Trust me; that role is needed as well.

It Was Always There

When I became the volunteer coordinator at one of my son's schools, I connected a passion for helping people with my gifts of administration. Assuming this type of role actually dates back to when I was in college, but I didn't realize it at the time. While serving as an assistant Girl Scout troop leader, I noticed the bridge at our campground needed repair. Being the outreach and social coordinator for our student chapter of the Society of Petroleum Engineers, I orchestrated a project where my classmates and I camped out and fixed the bridge. Not only were the girls in my troop grateful, but all the neighboring troops who used that campground benefited. The clothing drive after the trip to Africa reawakened my spirit of giving.

When Tiffany, one of my *What's Your Catalyst?* workshop participants, first arrived at the workshop, she felt fulfilled in her career in IT, and she had a balanced home life. She discovered through the activities, though, that she had an untapped longing to support young women in science, technology, engineering, and mathematics (STEM). As a result of the workshop, she joined forces with a local nonprofit dedicated to promoting STEM education to girls of color between the ages of seven to seventeen. As a result of her involvement, Tiffany helped hundreds of minority girls discover the benefits of a STEM career, and because of her commitment in finding her catalyst, she is committed to serving hundreds more.

Show Them How

As I led change in my community, I also found purpose in teaching others how to do so. As the volunteer coordinator for a couple of schools and the youth ministry program at my church, I found that I had created a set of repeatable steps that could benefit anyone in a volunteer coordinator position. Before long, I started teaching my processes to other servant leaders. Not only was I giving them important skills and tools, but I was also reinforcing my own understanding of how to use them. The simplified project-management processes in the Four-Step Strategic Change Leadership model proved their value in a variety of community organizations.

CHAPTER 18

Lead Change in Your Organization

• • •

By identifying your catalyst and applying its power to managing the change in your life and career, you can then lead change in your organization. Businesses are changing rapidly, and those who can keep pace with these changes get ahead. Being able to adapt is one of the key differentiators between successful and unsuccessful professionals and businesses (remember Blockbuster?). As you continue to grow in your career, ensure that you adapt your skills and mind-set to the demands of the industry and that you influence others to do the same.

Effective leaders empower their teams to grow, develop, and think independently. Their passion is contagious and spreads to people around them. The transformative power of knowing your purpose, passion, and priorities also makes you a beacon of light for others on your team and in your entire organization.

When you review your sphere of influence, you may feel that you are limited to your team or department. You may have limited authority, but you have almost unlimited influence. Influence is relational, and every time you interact with someone, you have the chance to influence their thoughts and behavior. For this reason, effective leaders understand that it's unwise to remain in a silo. It is also limited thinking to assume that because something is outside your department, you can't influence it.

While still establishing myself in the oil-field technology giant, I found myself positioned down the hall from key decision makers. The project that I had led successfully around North America was now being funded by another, more powerful group, and that meant I was part of the global headquarters. This group of mostly male, expatriate, executive-level managers welcomed me in and respected my professional advice on implementation strategy and technology. But it was when I was afforded the opportunity to share my experience as a woman field engineer to the director of human resources that I realized I had been positioned to speak up for other women. I was not a decision maker, but my proximity to several of them gave me the opportunity to affect change in policies.

This was the first example of seeing how my purpose and position worked hand in hand. When I began to envision my future and the type of change leader I wanted to be, I reflected on how small I felt around such senior managers but how big my impact was by speaking up. I imagined how much more impact I could have if I were elevated in the organization. That's just what I did; as my sphere of influence grew, my ability to impact change grew as well. I went from volunteering to recruit engineers to championing diversity and inclusion initiatives for women and minorities, even though my role had nothing to do with it. The shared responsibility I felt for the success of others in my life and career was cultivated in those initiatives.

Each time I was led by my catalyst, I found that I had influence that I didn't anticipate, whether I was on the team or leading the charge. Being a change leader is about seeing a need and finding the most constructive approach to meeting it. If you don't like your organization's culture, change it!

When Hurricane Katrina hit New Orleans in 2005, my home-town of Houston responded to the call to help the evacuees, and I was determined to be part of the solution. I volunteered with my company to revitalize an elementary school that would receive a large number of displaced residents. When I returned to my office, I saw a survey about corporate stewardship, and I responded immediately. Just like a voter in a local, state, or national election, I made my voice heard by contributing to the conversation. I've heard it said that hate is not the opposite of love—apathy is. As an employee or member of your organization, as a citizen of your nation, or as a leader in your family, you demonstrate your devotion by your actions.

When You Own the Organization

Once I formed my consulting firm in 2006, the organization I could influence most was my own. I used the Four-Step Strategic Change Leadership model to lead my own development as a business owner.

As my business grew, I was able to create opportunities by building a team. Creating a corporate culture where work-life balance, philanthropy, and the delivery of excellent client results were equally important wasn't an idealistic model; it was a necessity. Remaining true to my values was the key to my success. By applying the Decide, Devise, Do, and Review steps, I was able to continue to grow my business and impact an organization I established. Even more, with each engagement, I was able to impact my clients.

Mentor Emerging Leaders

As you grow in your professional leadership, you want to be on the lookout for opportunities to mentor other leaders. These may be people in your workplace, or they may be members of professional associations you belong to. They may even be in your neighborhood!

I am humbled every time I get a request from a friend or colleague to talk to their college-age child. Entrusting me to impart a few words of wisdom to another generation allows me to walk in my purpose. These same opportunities present themselves in professional associations, where I have the benefit of experience that some members may not yet have. Being able to provide advice helps their growth and also reinforces my understanding of particular issues. As your iron gets sharper, be intentional about finding opportunities to sharpen someone else's iron.

Conclusion

...

I often refer to my audit trip to Africa as an accidental mission trip, but in June of 2016, I had a chance to embark on an intentional mission trip to Honduras with my church. The planned seven days of assisting in a children's vacation Bible school, building a swing set, and providing medical missions were designed to leave a lasting impact on a community that felt forgotten. Aside from the smiles and squeals that I heard from the children all week, the highlight was being able to go there with my husband, Rodney, and our youngest son, Matthew.

The mission trip to Honduras was the first of many that we will take together to be catalysts for change in hearts beyond our normal reach. Unlike the wavering "OK, I'll go" for the trip to Africa, I jumped with a resounding yes to go to Honduras. Knowing my catalyst gave me boldness.

How Will You Use Your Catalyst?

So many things happen in life that are beyond our control. It's what we do with those things that we can control that make the difference in our success. It is my hope that after reading this book and responding to the questions, you have clarity on how purpose and passion can impact your life and leadership. The four sections work together to create a cohesive approach to drive strategic life change:

- **Know Yourself.** When you know yourself and reflect honestly on who you are and who you were made to be, you will recognize the direction you want to take. Understanding your purpose, passions, and priorities will guide you as you look forward.

- **Make a Strategic Plan.** Creating change in your life requires innovation, foresight, and careful planning, which are all talents that project professionals utilize regularly. Imagine what could happen when you use those same abilities for your self-development and growth. Simplified, it comes down to four steps: Decide, Devise, Do, and Review.

- **Keep Your Focus.** In order to realize the goals you established and to sustain their results, you have to minimize distractions and be mindful of other areas of your life that may hinder your focus. You have to be intentional to maintain your personal priorities.

- **Sharpen Someone Else**. Iron sharpens iron, and diamonds cut diamonds. As you are growing into the leader you aspire to be, find opportunities to share your knowledge and insights with others. Doing so will strengthen your understanding of key areas, and it will benefit others in the process. Leading and influencing others will add accountability to your journey, and it will reinforce your purpose.

In addition to reading the book, I want you to fully utilize the online resources at www.WhatsYourCatalyst.com to formulate a strategic plan to create and sustain those changes.

Whether you are leading change at home, in your organization, or in your community, you will want to do so with an equal emphasis on why, what, and how. Now that you know your catalyst, you can harness the power of managed change!

About the Author

. . .

Alana M. Hill is an international change leadership expert, inspiring professionals to lead change in their lives and their organizations. She is a passionate energy-industry veteran who has paved the way for women leaders behind her. Her experience as an engineer and certified PMP in IT and talent development provides real-world insight into how people and teams can excel, even in the face of adversity. Throughout her career, Alana has led diverse teams and delivered high-impact workshops all over the world!

With extensive cross-functional leadership and training expertise, Alana helps individuals and organizations accomplish their goals by utilizing sharp analysis, strategic planning, and interpersonal skills development. She promotes behavior styles and conflict resolution techniques to improve team dynamics and performance. Alana provides her clients with a combination of critical thinking and compassionate leadership, which she labels "Leading Change the Ms. Engineer Way." Her clients have included Fortune 500 companies, small technology companies, churches, and non-profits. Her adaptability makes her an asset across the professional spectrum.

Alana is available for speaking and training for businesses, organizations, and associations. Please visit www.TheMsEngineerWay.com.to see video, topics and to book Alana for your next event.

Notes

. . .

This book was based on years of research and experience as a project-and change management practitioner. Through leading, I've determined several best practices for establishing priorities, getting buy-in, and exceling even in the face of adversity. And while my own insights are important and valuable, I also relied on the research and expertise of several trusted resources. A few of them are listed below as valuable resources for you.

PMBOK 2017: *A Guide to the Project Management Body of Knowledge*, Sixth Edition, copyright the Project Management Institute, . All rights reserved.

Extended DISC is a registered trademark of Extended DISC NA, Inc.

Covey, Stephen R. 2016. *The 7 Habits of Highly Effective People*. FranklinCovey.

Further information on Project Management Professional (PMP) certification and the Project Management Institute (PMI) can be found at www.pmi.org.

Made in the USA
Lexington, KY
27 October 2019

56110572R00072